A Penguin Special
Under Siege

Keith Tompson was born in 1954 in :
He received an honours degree in politics and sociology, and studied
for a Ph.D., at the University of Kent. He joined Workers Against
Racism on its formation in 1979 and was the East London organizer
from 1981 to 1983. He was then a lecturer at Birmingham Poly-
technic until 1984. Since 1985 Keith Tompson has been National
Organizer of Workers Against Racism. A founder member of the
Revolutionary Communist Party (1981), he contributes regularly to
its weekly newspaper, *The Next Step*. He is the author of *The Roots
of Racism* (1985, 1986).

Keith Tompson

Under Siege

Racism and Violence in Britain Today

FOREWORD BY JOHN PILGER

PENGUIN BOOKS

PENGUIN BOOKS

Published by the Penguin Group
27 Wrights Lane, London W8 5TZ, England
Viking Penguin Inc., 40 West 23rd Street, New York, New York 10010, USA
Penguin Books Australia Ltd, Ringwood, Victoria, Australia
Penguin Books Canada Ltd, 2801 John Street, Markham, Ontario, Canada L3R 1B4
Penguin Books (NZ) Ltd, 182–190 Wairau Road, Auckland 10, New Zealand

Penguin Books Ltd, Registered Offices: Harmondsworth, Middlesex, England

First published 1988
10 9 8 7 6 5 4 3 2 1

Made and printed in Great Britain by Richard Clay Ltd, Bungay, Suffolk
Filmset in Monophoto Plantin

This book is for my mother Iris,
who is always telling me to get a proper job.
I believe she may now think that I have
found the right one.

Contents

Preface

When I completed the manuscript for *Under Siege*, in February 1988, London's Camden Council had, through its policy of singling out the 'intentionally homeless', in effect refused to house Asian and Irish families and begun a policy that would send them back to their country of origin. Camden argued that, though a Labour-controlled local authority, it could not provide housing for such people. This, to me, seemed a warning of what was to come and the end of the line for what I will describe in this book as municipal anti-racism. If there was any doubt about it then, the report into the killing of Ahmed Iqbal, at Burnage High School in Manchester, further confirmed that municipal anti-racism has fuelled the fires of racial hatred: the opposite of its intention.

In November 1987 the Conservative government had announced a new Bill on immigration, aimed at repatriating Asian males. By preventing Asian men from bringing their wives and children to Britain, it demanded that they either go to where they had come from or live a life separate from their families.

These episodes sum up the problems of the moment. The round-up of foreigners – for that, unfortunately, is indeed what we are witnessing today – has finally arrived. It is a worrying time for black people. Those opposed to racism are trapped in a strategy that only adds to the problem.

How, in a period of growing racial harassment, backed by both local and national government, can an effective response to racism be prepared? I believe that what is needed is nothing less than a massive new anti-racist movement, independent of officialdom and uncompromising in its defence of black people. Thus, while this book may offer encouragement to

Britain's black community and show its members that they are not alone, I hope above all that it will result in many new applications to join such a movement. These applications, and they alone, will decide whether *Under Siege* is a success or a failure.

It is traditional in a preface to thank those who have helped to prepare the book. There are many debts to be acknowledged. I owe a debt first to Kennan Malik, who is a regular contributor to *The Next Step* and did most of the research for chapter 4. I would also like to thank others who have served as an inspiration for many of the ideas in the book, namely Frank Richards, Joan Phillips and James Wood. Only their previous work, their availability for constant discussion and their patience have made *Under Siege* possible. It was John Pilger who originally encouraged me to take on this project; and his interest in the book has matched his concern for the victims of racism themselves; I am most grateful for it. Finally, I would like to thank Jon Riley at Penguin for patiently awaiting the final manuscript and for his sound advice on its construction, and Gemma Forest for editing my semi-literate English into its present form.

I should point out that the use of the word 'black' in the book refers to all non-whites and thus includes Asian people and others affected by racism.

Foreword

by John Pilger

On the night of 25 January 1982 a gang of forty attacked the
home of the Saddique family in the East End of London.
They threw stones, smashing the shop windows and narrowly
missing the family crouched inside in darkness. They daubed
swastikas, gave Nazi salutes and chanted, 'Fucking Pakis out!'
They did this for six straight hours without intervention
from the police. Nasreen, the eldest daughter, then aged 14,
wrote in her diary: 'When the trouble started, we phone the
police, but they never came. Then again we phone the police,
but they never came. Then my father went to the police
station to get the police; we had a witness. The police said
they didn't need a witness.'

The entries in Nasreen's diary for the days, weeks, months
and years that followed, often written by candlelight or in
freezing darkness as the family huddled in an upstairs room,
were repetitive and to the point: 'Trouble. Got no sleep.
Three or four of them throw stones at our window.' The
'three or four' would sit outside and watch for movement.
Then shit would be smeared on the front door, then there
would be more rocks, then an uncertain silence until dawn.

For most of these six years the Saddiques have stayed
together in their one large room overlooking the street. They
seldom go outside after seven o'clock at night; neither do
they go downstairs after dark. Only their dog, a worrying
beast called Soldier, is downstairs in the front room that
used to be the father's tailor shop and until recently was bar-
ricaded at the urging of the police, who say they can do
nothing.

I have become a close friend and adviser of the Saddiques.

Our friendship is conducted mostly by phone. Seldom a week passes when I do not speak to Nasreen. She is the voice of her parents, who came to Britain from Pakistan twenty-one years ago. The conversations with Nasreen run to a pattern. 'Nasreen 'ere,' she says in her Cockney accent. 'They're at the door now. Hear 'em? I've called the police and they're comin', *so they say*. That's all. 'Bye.'

She may ring back to say they are all right. She may ask me to ring Newham Council the next day, and occasionally the police that night, but usually she asks nothing; she is merely making contact with the world outside her barricade. She reminds me of Anne Frank, the Jewish girl who hid in the attic of her home in Amsterdam during the Nazi occupation and kept a diary of her life. That the analogy is not at all far-fetched ought to be enough to prompt decent people to reflect anxiously upon the political nature of the society in which we now live.

Keith Tompson begins his important book with the Saddiques' story and is right to do so for it is both shocking and typical. In the late 1980s racist attacks in London have reached a level reminiscent of that of the violence against Jews during the early part of the century. I have yet to meet an Asian family in the East End who has not been subjected to constant, casual brutality, ranging from the daily tormenting of children to petrol-bombing, and I have yet to meet a black person under siege who has been adequately protected by the police or given sustained support by the authorities. Keith Tompson refers to the sheaf of letters that Nasreen Saddique has written to politicians – from Margaret Thatcher to her Labour MP – as well as to her local council and others. Their responses, such as they are, have changed nothing. She received one letter from the Home Office that, in its unguarded honesty, urged her to keep reporting every attack to the police 'even if the police are unable to take effective action'.

Nasreen refuses to give up. Many others refuse to give up. Keith Tompson is one of them. I met Keith in the early

1980s through Workers Against Racism, then and now the only organized group in London offering twenty-four-hour protection and support to families under siege.

It was Keith and the other young men and women of Workers Against Racism, black and white, who camped on the floor of the Saddiques' home and perhaps saved their lives. It was Keith and his comrades who protected a single Bangladeshi father with three children on an all-white council estate and, through remarkable skill and patience, isolated the racists on the estate and mobilized decent people against them. 'We canvassed every home on his 500-dwelling estate,' writes Keith. 'We discovered more than 300 anti-racists. Of these thirty were invited to private meetings. We explained what had happened and asked for their help . . . The attacks on Mr Ali stopped as rapidly as they had begun . . . The racists have become the outcasts.'

I know Mr Ali. I remember his account of the first attack on his children, by a man with a frothing German Shepherd dog. When the police turned up, after an interminable delay, they demanded to see Mr Ali's rent book to check that he was 'legal' – that is, legally entitled to be in Britain – which he was. Then they left. Nobody was arrested; nobody was cautioned.

Most families under siege are simply too terrified to call the police for fear of being prosecuted themselves. This is not, as some might say, an anti-police observation. Police behaviour in cases of racial violence is well documented – as, indeed, are police attitudes and the political encouragement they receive. The evidence is in the pages of this book.

What is so compelling about Keith Tompson's investigation and analysis, not to mention his fine Swiftian anger, is that it spares no shibboleth: for example, that racism is endemic in white working-class people. At its inception, he writes, racism was the property only of a patriotic elite. It was the rise of the nation-state, seeking ever expanding markets, and, with it, the rise of patriotism that gave 'the vocabulary and culture of racism a systematic form', and it was the oppression of colonial peoples that gave 'nationalism its racist form'.

Certainly when I was growing up in a far corner of the British Empire, racism and imperialism were indivisible. The fairytales of racial superiority that were poured into my head at school and elsewhere came from one source. Thus the *Encyclopaedia Britannica* could inform me that the black man in Australia was 'an animal of prey and more ferocious than the lynx, the leopard, or the hyena [and] devours his own species'. This was typical of the nonsense that had justified the dispossession and slaughter of an indigenous people by patriotic Christian gentlemen seeking to 'open up' a continent and its 'natural wealth', which they had 'discovered'.

·The same notions of patriotism justifying racism were expressed in another guise and to great effect by one Enoch Powell, who always seemed to me to embody the colonial experience reproduced in Britain. I spent part of an election campaign in the Midlands with Powell, in his black Homburg and pre-war pinstripes. His bitter longing for the 'lost' Raj of India (which he had served) permeated almost every speech he made about race. At one noisy rally in Wolverhampton a Sikh man asked him with courage and some deference, 'Mr Powell, if you are again in a position of power, will you move to send us and our children out of this country?'

With that, Powell's aloofness and his affectation of Churchill-in-the-wilderness collapsed. Moving to the edge of the platform, jabbing his finger down at the questioner, he bellowed, 'Listen, my man, *this* is not your country, nor your children's country. Your place in human society was set for you and was right where you came from – and that's where you should be!'

This utterly crude and vindictive side of Powell was then not often represented in the press and that is certainly still true today. If anything, Powell has been legitimized as the racism of government has become more and more overt and shameless, as people are regularly killed, maimed, sacked, deported and imprisoned because of their ethnic origins. At the time of writing, the twentieth anniversary of Powell's 'rivers of blood' speech is being celebrated by much of the British press, and not merely in the tabloids – and 'celebrated' is the correct word. An article in the *Independent* is headed 'Enoch Powell, midwife to the spirit of the nation'. Alas, in one sense I would not contest the accuracy of that.

I hope that the promoters of such fashionable, effete views of Powell, those who praise his constitutional stands and his intellect, will read this book. They then may reflect that the incidence and severity of racist attacks, including murder, are closely related to the type of mass resentment that Powell and other respectable propagandists, especially the instigators of 'immigration scares', have stirred so successfully.

I was in Kenya in 1968 to report one such 'scare'. In response to Conservative baiting that the Labour government was 'soft' on immigration – rather like accusing the United States Congress of being soft on communism – the Home Secretary, James Callaghan, hurried through a draconian Immigration Bill that took away people's nationality and the value of their British passports and was unabashed in its racial motivation. This caused the stampede of thousands of Asian people whose forebears had been shipped *en masse* to East Africa to service the British Empire. At Nairobi Airport I joined in rescuing children caught underfoot in the panic. Uncertainty and fear had been dispensed at great distance and without immediate responsibility. Callaghan went on to become Prime Minister.

Perhaps the most interesting analysis in this book derives from the author's trenchant criticisms of those whom he calls 'municipal anti-racists'. 'Today,' he writes, 'the great majority of anti-racist groups in east London are on the payroll of a local council.' He castigates those Labour councils that do not just 'divert' people from tackling racial violence but actively 'deter' them from doing so. 'While councils did battle against "unconscious racism", all too conscious racists waged a real war on black people. In 1986 a quarter of Newham's Asian population suffered racist attacks, yet the council responded by creating a special "hit squad" to remove racist graffiti and by sending its housing staff on yet more anti-racist training courses.' He also contends that by allowing a genuine anti-racist like the teacher Maureen McGoldrick to be pilloried for allegedly making racist remarks (after a governor's inquiry had cleared her), Brent Council actually caused a hardening of racist attitudes in the community and exposed black people to more violence.

I accept the logic of that, but I cannot share all of Keith's strictures on those local authorities that, with ever-dwindling resources, at least have *tried* to attack the roots of racism: the 'consciousness' and the vocabulary. They may not have done this very well; they may even at times be 'silly', as he says; but they have occupied, and they still occupy, ground that would have been submerged by the tide of racist authoritarianism.

That London councils such as Camden, which have been denied the right to spend community money on housing and basic services, should now be offering people air tickets as an alternative to homes says more about the success of Thatcherism than about their own indecency. And if black and anti-racist groups had not been supported by the GLC and by Labour authorities, what would have become of them?

However, Keith is right when he takes issue with councils and the Commission for Racial Equality over their policy of priority transfer for victims of racial attack. This represents an insidious defeatism. For example, whenever an Asian shopkeeper I know is attacked by thugs, he is urged by the police to close down his business and move on. But why should he? Why should the racists win? Various officials have wanted the Saddique family to move on; yet it is only in recent months that Newham Council has moved to get rid of the mini-cab office next door that has been a prime source of the family's suffering. And there is the example of Mr Ali, whom Tower Hamlets wanted to move on. He and his children now live in peace on a once notorious estate because the initiative was taken away from the racists by bold, radical community action that *worked*. Moreover it would not have worked had there not already existed a base of goodwill among ordinary people, who, unlike the elites, are a living part of this multi-racial society.

It is this positive vision of this book that I much appreciate. Keith tells a number of stories similar to Mr Ali's, in which white working people have been persuaded that they are not the beneficiaries of racism and that by standing up both to organized and insidious racism, they too are strengthened.

I believe that, in spite of the silence of many of the media, people *are* aware that authoritarianism is accelerating in Britain, that fragile freedoms are being lost. At present black people just happen to be at the dirtiest end of a stick being wielded across racial lines, but that is changing, and changing fast, as the judiciary and state violence are used more and more to subdue those who are struggling for a livelihood and who are not black.

With the Thatcher 'revolution' virtually unopposed in Parliament and by the institutions, British politics are nothing if not volatile. And people are never still. In 1984, when the South Wales Striking Miners' Choir entertained an entirely black audience in Walsall, one of the choristers paid tribute to the 'ethnic minorities' who had been so outstanding in their support during the strike. To which a black leader responded, 'The Welsh are the ethnic minority in Walsall!' And both audience and choristers stood and cheered. 'The strike,' said the writer Hywel Francis, who recounted this story, 'has begun to teach all of us that none of us are minorities.'

Introduction

In the Thirties it was the Jews. Now it is Pakistanis who are the victims of racial violence in London's East End in a wave of thuggery and intimidation. Many are even afraid to go out to work. They have good reason to fear.

Scarcely a week passes without another racial attack. On women and children as well as men. Sometimes in broad daylight.

They are attacked on the streets and in their homes. Air guns are fired at them. They are beaten up. Blazing rags are pushed through letter boxes. The windows of their shops and clubs are smashed.[1]

It is not only on the streets of London that these horrific incidents now take place in Britain. On 17 September 1986 Ahmed Iqbal, a 13-year-old Bangladeshi boy from the Manchester area, was brutally stabbed in the playground of his school. Iqbal died in a police car on the way to hospital.

The day before, Iqbal had gone to the defence of another Bangladeshi boy who had been under threat from racist attackers. One attacker told him, 'I will get you tomorrow, you Paki.' His killing the following day was a premeditated racist murder. His sister, Selina, explains: 'On Monday my brother defended a Bengali boy from being bullied. On Tuesday the bullies picked a fight with my brother, but they came off the worse. On Wednesday the bully picked another fight with my brother, but this time he stabbed him.'[2]

Iqbal's father has had a heart attack and is seriously ill as a result of the shock. Iqbal's sister postponed her marriage because she has had to look after her grieving parents. Another sister has had to give up her place at Lancaster University. The attack has devastated the entire family.

Iqbal's murder was part of a pattern that reaches back over

a decade. In 1978 Altab Ali was stabbed by racists and left in a gutter in east London's Whitechapel Road; later Ishaque Ali was bludgeoned to death on the streets of Hackney. In August 1979 Kayimarz Anklesaria was kicked to death at Bromley-by-Bow Tube station, east London. The following summer Akhtar Ali Baig was stabbed in broad daylight in East Ham. In February 1981 racists wrecked the Hindu temple in Coventry's Stoney Stanton area. That same year skinheads in Coventry stabbed a young Asian, Satnam Singh Gill, to death. In Walthamstow, north-east London, Mrs Khan and her three young children lost their lives in a fire-bomb attack on their home. Two years into Margaret Thatcher's first term as Prime Minister the streets of Britain's major cities were not safe for Asians to walk or live on.

By the mid 1980s reported attacks on black people in east London had more than doubled. In Newham reported attacks rose from seventy-seven in 1982 to 146 by 1984; in 1987 it was estimated that one in four of the borough's Asian community had been the victim of a racial attack, and even police reports acknowledged that there were 188 attacks in a year.[3] The figure for London as a whole was 960 reported racist attacks.[4]

These figures record only those attacks that have been reported to the police. They drastically underestimate how bad things have become for black people in and around east London. In July 1984 West Indian railman Peter Burns was racially abused by commuters, then murdered when a metal stake was pushed through his eye. Three months later a halal butcher's shop in Newham was blown to pieces by an enormous bomb, while another Asian shopkeeper's car exploded when he turned on the ignition. In July 1985 Shamira Kassam, a pregnant woman, died with her three small sons in a firebomb attack on her home in Ilford, Essex. 'Under siege' may seem a melodramatic way of describing the plight of black people in Britain today. But, as the Home Office admitted early on in 1981, racially motivated attacks are common, on the increase and fifty or sixty times more likely to happen to black people than to whites.[5] Black people really *are* under siege – and not just by local racists but also by employers, the police, the courts and the immigration authorities.

1   *The public and racial violence*

On 14 January 1987 the Metropolitan Police issued a special pamphlet for victims of racial harassment. The advice included the following:

> If you find your windows are constantly being smashed, you could replace the glass with reinforced plastic. This makes them less dangerous . . . On returning home late at night, have your house keys ready to let yourself in quickly . . . Don't encourage peeping toms! Draw your curtains at night and remove clothes from your outside line . . . Keep a dog . . . Never walk home alone at night . . . Keep your hands out of your pockets . . . If you are cornered or threatened, try and attract attention by screaming and shouting. If you're actually attacked, you can fight back using anything to hand, such as an umbrella or your shoes.[1]

The Met's advice is of little relevance to the victims of racist attack. It simply amounts to a demand that black people look after themselves. It holds the victim, and nobody else, responsible for defending life and limb.

Umbrellas and shoes are of little use against knife-wielding attackers who roam in gangs and attack at random. Yet this is but the first of many examples we shall find of society turning its back on the needs of black people. As we shall see, the experiences of the Saddique and Lone families, and of Trevor Ferguson, suggest that black people do not need the Met's kind of advice. Self-defence comes naturally to those under attack. What is needed is a way of stopping the attacks in the first place.

The Saddique family

John Pilger, writing in the *Independent*, presented a catalogue of racial violence against east London's black community. Of the Saddiques he said:

Last week Nasreen phoned me to say: 'We have a new neighbour who is nice to us. We are taking down the barriers and we are hoping for the best; but we are frightened.'

I have known Nasreen and her family for four years and this is the first good news. Almost every night since 25 January 1982 they have stayed together in their one large room, overlooking their street in the East End of London. They seldom go out after seven o'clock at night, neither do they go downstairs after dark.[2]

Nasreen has many tales to tell. The following is about an occasion in 1982, soon after she and her family had moved into their new home.

There was a violent knock at the front door and an enormous crash against the boarded-up window. Voices echoed through the letter-box: 'Fucking Pakis.' I was upstairs peering through the bedroom curtain, lights out, hoping it wouldn't be like the previous night, hoping they would disappear into the darkness and leave me and my parents alone.

Experience told me that it was unlikely. This had been happening every night for weeks. There seemed to be no end to it all.

Nasreen Saddique is a young Asian woman who, together with her family, has been living under siege for almost six years. She is now 20 years old but was a young 14 when I was first called to her home in the early months of 1982. The family had just moved into a new house in the West Ham district of east London. They had chosen the house because it had a shop-front downstairs: there was thus space both for living accommodation and for a business.

The house was part of a circle of houses with a small park in the middle. Next door on one side was a mini-cab office and, on the other, a pub. Opposite was a newsagent and other retail traders. The houses were three storeys high, providing plenty of room. Nasreen shared the house with her parents and her sister and two brothers. Her parents' bed-room, on the first floor, overlooked the park. Nasreen's room lay above it.

The Saddiques hoped to decorate the ground floor and open a business but, from day one they were subject to persistent harassment. A gang of youths would congregate in the park and shout abuse, often throwing projectiles and smashing the windows of the ground floor. It was only days before the entire ground floor window had to be boarded up. Nasreen's mother began a nightly vigil from her bed overlooking the park, waiting for trouble.

The police and the council seemed unprepared to help. Something had to be done. Mrs Saddique is an asthmatic, and throughout her six years of torment her condition has worsened to such a degree that, because of countless sleepless nights, she has to be admitted to hospital regularly. Mr Saddique has been unable to open a business.

My first visit to the Saddiques' home happened a few short weeks after they had moved in. I and other volunteers from East London Workers Against Racism (ELWAR) became more or less a permanent feature for the Saddiques. For them, as for many familes in east London, we were very much a last resort.

Formed in 1979 by members of the Revolutionary Communist Party, ELWAR was a response to a wave of murders of Asians in Tower Hamlets and Newham. At the time the Anti-Nazi League had gained a temporary popularity by focusing on pockets of fascists, replying to them with its famous 'Rock against Racism' concerts. ELWAR, by contrast, had a broader, more practical aim. It focused on a less histrionic but more widespread problem – racism. It worked to give the victims of racism physical support when they encountered difficulty.

ELWAR achieved some rapid successes in dealing with racial violence. By 1982 we had won a name for our efficient protection of families and individuals under attack. ELWAR's activities were described as 'vigilantism'; in reality, however, they were an attempt to bring white working-class people to the black community's aid. In addition, E L W A R's politics stressed the need not to be reliant on the police – a view that bitter experience had confirmed was right but that both Conservative and Labour politicians were quick to denounce.

Today, more than five years after we first came to their aid, the Saddiques are still under continual harassment. Nasreen now works for Newham Council, but her entire adolescent life has been scarred. For her, going through a racist assault is not unlike the experience of air-raids that east London families had during the Second World War. 'It's like living under a table,' she says. 'The whole time you're looking for where the next attack is coming from.'

Nasreen began to keep a diary of the attacks on her and her family. For a frightened but defiant young girl this was the only way to come to terms with what was going on. The diary now runs to some two hundred pages. Often repetitive, it nevertheless gives a gripping account of life under the table. Within a week of its commencement the diary recorded that fighting went on from 6.30 p.m. to midnight. From then on the story was the same: 26 January, 'Trouble. Got no sleep'; 27 January, 'Trouble. Got no sleep.' The diary tells a tale of police indifference and describes conditions in the street.

The mini-cab office next door to the Saddiques acted as a magnet for the racists. Its proprietor had installed space invaders machines as a way of supplementing his income, so the premises were full of young people who used them as a base from which to launch salvos against the family: 28 January, 'Every night we have to call the police but the police didn't do anything. Two youths kick our front door and went in the mini-cab office'; 29 January, 'My uncle came round and before he came there was trouble. My uncle came in and the youths were swearing. Three or four youths were standing in the church and they threw stones at our house and broke windows (three times). The police came four times and did nothing but told the youths to go away. When the windows were being broken, the glass just missed my father's head.'

The saga of the Saddiques is not a sensational one. They are still alive. There are hundreds of east London Pakistanis who have been through all their torments – and hundreds of thousands of blacks in Britain who have suffered some of their misery. But for them life is one long encirclement. Today Nasreen explains:

My mum is getting on. She is ill anyway, to the extent that she has a respirator by the side of her bed. She doesn't speak a lot of English, though she understands most things. The past six years have ruined her life, to the point where she can't sleep at night. During the evening she just sits at the window at the front of the house overlooking the trouble spot. She doesn't move from that window. My father will not venture out alone. Only a few weeks ago they stole his van during the night and smashed it up.

As soon as their Calvary began, the Saddiques asked local politicians and local police to do something. Eventually they took their case to 10 Downing Street. At every stage the responses they encountered revealed a lot about official complacency towards racial attacks. It is not that the British authorities *do not know* about the treatment black people receive from white racists. It is, rather, that they *do not want to know*.

One month after first moving into Newham Nasreen wrote to her local Labour MP, Arthur Lewis, to tell him what had been happening: how the police had failed to come to her family's assistance, how a crowd of about forty people would gather outside her house, how problems had arisen every single night. Mr Lewis's reply, on 16 February 1982, was to the point:

Of course I express my sympathy and understanding of your problem and condemn unreservedly all concerned in these fascist activities. You will readily appreciate that this is a police matter and I have no power or control over the police. All that I can do . . . is to call upon the police for a report and action upon these matters. I will keep you posted upon developments.

Disheartened by this response, Nasreen once more applied to Lewis for help. Three weeks on, in a lengthy plea, she noted:

Since we last wrote to you things have got worse. One evening a group of youths painted NF [National Front] slogans all over our door. Lots of youths on motorbikes drive past the house all the time, shouting and making lots of noise. Our door is always being kicked and stones are still being thrown at the windows and at the doors. The police have not done anything at all and we are frightened that the attacks will get worse until finally we will have petrol bombs thrown.

When we came to this house we did not think that we would be treated like this. I don't think we can live like this any more – I don't think my mother and father can stand it any more.

You are the only person who can help us now – we have no one else to turn to. The attacks are just going to carry on getting worse and worse and no one is doing anything to help us – so we are relying on you.

We would also like you to come and visit us to see what state we are living in – or if you cannot come personally, we would like you to send someone on your behalf. My mother and father are very depressed because no one seems to be really concerned about what is happening to us. You are our last hope.[3]

Lewis's response was to repeat the points contained in his first letter, to promise again to raise the matter with the police and to refer to the family's difficulties not as racial harassment but as a run-of-the-mill housing matter. Nasreen's reply was forthright:

We have written to you twice and both times you have nicely avoided our problem.

The police seem to come only when you either phone them or write to them or when they feel they are being watched by people such as you. Since the attacks began, they have failed to arrest one person. And now they rarely turn up even once a week.

You say in your letter that our problem is housing. We have a house, Mr Lewis, and we want to stay in the house. But these kids won't let us – so please don't avoid us in that way.

I again ask for your help. To come and visit us and see what our problem exactly is. To ask your local Labour Party members to defend us. About 14 people have died this year, Mr Lewis, by attacks on Asian houses.

I hope you will respond to my letter and take up my suggestion.

In the end the tenacity of a 15-year-old girl ensured that what had been a local affair was transformed into a House of Commons issue – one discussed, indeed, by Mrs Thatcher herself. But while Arthur Lewis used his parliamentary position to gain a high public profile over the Saddiques, he continued with his previous stance in private:

Whilst I can fully understand and appreciate your concern it is not true to say that I have avoided your problem because previously and now I have explained the FACT that the question of the enforcement of the law rests with the police and I have no power, control, say, voice or influence in any way whatsoever over their actions (or inactions). I have raised this matter in the House of Commons and with the police and like you I regret that they are so dilatory and lacksaidasical [sic] that they do not take any action.[4]

The Saddiques were fortified by the publicity they had gained, but, as Nasreen told Lewis in a letter, the Commons discussion had 'little consequence' for them.[5] What had a much more direct effect, both on the family and on Arthur Lewis, was the intervention of ELWAR. After she had invited him to a meeting that ELWAR had organized on her behalf Lewis told Nasreen:

I am afraid that due to a very long-standing prior engagement it will not prove possible for me to attend the meeting to which you make reference and whilst I am in no way suggesting that it is the case in this instance, I am usually rather loth to attend some meetings which are called to exascerbate [sic] and inflame genuine and proper grievances and matters of complaint for ulterior and sometimes wrong political motives. I repeat that I am not suggesting that this is the case in this instance, but I always take great care to see that offers of help and support are made for genuine reason of trying to resolve the problems rather than to 'increase difficulties' and to 'stir up' problems for the purpose of gaining political advantages.[6]

When, in 1983, Newham North West saw Tony Banks take over from Arthur Lewis as its local MP, the Saddiques were full of hope. Unlike Lewis, Banks visited the family in person. In September 1983, however, Banks told the family that it would be best for them to move and, like his predecessor, spoke of a housing problem rather than one of racial violence. Then in April 1984, after drivers from the mini-cab agency had themselves begun to harass the Saddiques, Banks wrote:

I sympathize with the problem you have over the mini-cab firm, and I will raise this with the police. However, the basis of the problem lies in the fact that your street is only partly residential and therefore actually more suitable for a mini-cab firm than most streets in Newham, and while it is operating there will always be a conflict of interest.

I realize how hard it is for you to be in the middle of all this, but despite the fact that your family does have a genuine grievance, your parents are going to have to make some hard decisions about moving.[7]

One year later, after more attacks, Banks wrote:

Minor infractions of the bye-laws regarding noise do not give sufficient excuse or reason to the Council or the Police to act except in a fairly ineffective way.

He concluded:

You believe the mini-cab firm are still making life difficult for you, while the Council and the Police say there is very little evidence to back this up, given that Church Street North is not an ideal residential area and is in fact fairly suitable for a mini-cab firm to operate from.[8]

Like Lewis before him, Banks tried to alter the terms of the argument. In fact, his whole argument – that the family was living on a commercial street – was bogus. About twelve months after Banks's letter Newham Council itself allowed houses to be built opposite the Saddiques' home. What had really been happening was this: two Labour MPs had made a succession of polite attempts to persuade a young girl to influence her parents to move – for the simple reason that her parents were Asian.

Nasreen next wrote to Mrs Thatcher. The reply she received came not from the Prime Minister but from the Home Office. Unlike the police, the Home Office acknowledged that attacks were indeed taking place and that they were racially inspired. It spoke of the family's 'continuing troubles' and the harassment suffered. The Home Office's letter concluded: 'I am sorry that I am not able to give a more helpful reply, but let me take this opportunity to assure you that the government does care about the incidence of racial attacks and is committed to a multi-racial society in which we all can go without fear of racial violence or abuse.'[9]

This statement says everything about British officialdom's attitude to racial violence. Quite simply, the attitude is 'tough luck'. It exemplifies why this country's police systematically fail to show up when the victims of a racist attack report one in progress. It explains why the Saddiques' nightmare has gone on.

Day in, day out, Nasreen's diary is full of the abuse she and her parents have received – of the sticks, the punches and the graffiti. On 7 July 1985 drivers from the mini-cab office throw litter inside the family's door and tell Mrs Saddique that litter is good for her. On 4 November 'They kick our van and start swearing at us and threaten us, saying, "We are going to put petrol down your letterbox."' Even today the Saddiques still have trouble with the mini-cab drivers. Although they have won a court order for the removal of the office, it has yet to go. Meanwhile, to make their lives even more tragic, new racists have appeared – the builders constructing the houses opposite them.

Throughout six years of intimidation and violence the

Saddiques have not persuaded the police or the council to take their problems seriously. On 6 April 1982, at West Ham police station, I attended a meeting at which Chief Inspector Ferguson added his voice to those suggesting that the street was not suitable for the Saddique family to live in. Three years later, in a letter to Tony Banks, Chief Superintendent Barrett wrote: 'The arrival of a demonstrative Asian family in a predominantly whites' playground area had unpleasant effects ... The cul-de-sac environment is unsuitable for peaceful residential purposes ... police do feel that there is a case for re-housing this family.'[10] Barrett only stated more boldly what everybody else had hinted at – that the Saddiques were to blame for their choice of a 'whites' playground' and that the solution to their problems was not for the racists to be made to desist but for the family to be uprooted.

Even more than Arthur Lewis, the police were concerned about ELWAR rather than racial attacks. On 9 February 1982 five ELWAR volunteers and an independent photographer were at the Saddiques' home. After the photographer had taken pictures of those responsible for harassing the family a van-load of police, called in by the attackers on the grounds that the Saddiques had 'strange people' in the house, piled into the family's property. 'I don't want any photos taken or I will arrest you all,' announced the officer in charge. He went on to say that his men were looking for 'strange people' and to warn the family not to have anything to do with ELWAR and its 'vigilantes'.

On 24 July 1985 Inspector Hoskin, from West Ham police, told Nasreen that her family should have expected all along that living next to a mini-cab office would lead to problems. He also told her to stop asking the journalist John Pilger to telephone the police on her behalf.

While the police tried to dissuade Nasreen from seeking to publicize the case, the council was not particularly helpful. In a letter to Tony Banks, Newham Council's Environmental Health Department deputy, A. J. Griffin, stated that the family's complaints 'had nothing to do with racial harassment' and that they were of 'relatively minor importance'.[11] Even now Nasreen's diary continues. It is a diary that Britain's Asians could duplicate many times over.

The Lone family

There's always attacks round here. Recently an Afro-Caribbean guy was attacked because he had a white girl with him, and two black guys were beaten up by a gang outside the fish-and-chip shop. The police ignored both incidents.

When Naeem and his dad were beaten up, I spoke to the sister at the Newham General emergency department. She said that no black person was safe on a Friday or a Saturday night along the Barking Road – every night she was sure to get a case, some so badly hurt you couldn't recognize them.

If the police really want to know about racist attacks, they should speak to the hospital emergency department.[12]

Like the Saddiques, the Lones live in Newham. Naeem is 17 years old and works in a London office of the Department of Health and Social Security. His father is Mubasha; his uncle, Ezaz Hayat, runs a Southern Fried Chicken fast-food shop on the Barking Road. The Barking Road area of Newham is a notorious scene of racial violence. Local gangs inhabit the streets and intimidate Asian pedestrians and businesses. There is a whole string of closed restaurants and shops, once owned by Asians. This is how Hayat describes life for black people in Barking Road:

There is no shop here which is free of trouble. One at a time, all the shops get it. At the moment it is mostly me.

When I opened the shop up about six months ago, they used to come in causing confusion, changing their orders, trying to steal off the counter, abusing us, saying, 'Hey, nigger/Paki, hurry up.' I used to speak to them and try to be friendly, but it was no good. They used to take food and run out without paying and leave less money than they should have paid.

Then they started threatening us, about sixteen to twenty of them, all white boys, but they get support from older brothers and fathers.

One day they gave the staff a lot of abuse. They didn't want to leave the shop and were asking us out for a fight. We told them to leave but they started throwing food about the shop.

We went outside . . . They started throwing things, and a few of them pulled out knives.[13]

Hayat manages the shop. Dalton Macauley, whose family are from Africa, co-owns it with him. From its opening in July 1986 onwards, the place has met with one disaster after another.

The southern stretch of Barking Road, from Canning Town docks up to Plaistow and East Ham, has long been a no-go area for blacks. For years the effect of Newham's Labour council's housing policy has been that the south of the borough is virtually white-only and that blacks are consigned to low-grade estates north of the Barking Road divide. Today the Croydon Road Gang still patrols the frontier between the two territories. It was on the Barking Road that the gang left its mark on Naeem and his father Mubasha.

In statements to the police Dalton Macauley takes up the story in the months following the opening of the shop. His account is worth quoting in full:

On Friday, 29 August, at about 12.30 a.m, we had finished trading and had locked up the shop and were just about to go home. I could see a number of youths standing on the opposite side of the Barking Road, near the off-licence. I went outside the shop and could also see a number of other youths standing in Croydon Road. I recognized those youths as having been banned from the shop because of the trouble they had caused in the past by coming to the shop, shouting racial abuse at me and threatening myself and the rest of the staff. When I went outside to have a look, they shouted at me: 'You black bastard, you come here.' I went back inside the shop where Mr Hayat, a friend and my younger brother was.

I then saw Jason Swale[14] come from Croydon Road, run across the Barking Road and then stand opposite the shop near Clove Street. I could see that he was carrying two bottles, one in each hand. Swale was wearing a black jacket and chequered trousers. I knew Jason Swale because he came into the shop every day over the last three months: he has blond, short, spiky hair, like a crewcut – he is quite distinctive. Swale then disappeared round the corner into Clove Street. I then came out of the shop into the Barking Road and the youths that were still in the street were shouting racial abuse at me. Swale then came running from the crowd: I could see that he had a milk bottle in his hand and that the top of it had a rag in it and that it was on fire. Swale then came into the middle of the Barking Road and threw the bomb towards the shop and myself. The bomb exploded on the pavement and in Braemor Road, about fifteen to twenty feet from myself. I saw the flames from the bomb go up and felt the heat from the fire. At that point I went back into the shop and locked the door. I was frightened for my safety.

At the junction of Barking Road and Clove Street, where the group of youths was standing, I saw Jimmy Smart. He was holding a milk bottle, which was on fire: he ran a few steps and threw the bomb, which exploded in the road. Smart was wearing a green jacket with a hood and blue jeans. I know Smart because he comes into the shop regularly and he has threatened me a number of times, and has also tried to run me down with a car. The group of youths were armed with sticks and, before the bombs were thrown, I saw Smart with a cricket bat in his hand.

On Friday, 19 September 1986, at about 10 p.m. I was working in the shop with Mr Hayat and there were about eight customers waiting to be served. A white youth came into the shop, aged about 18 to 20 years. He had fair hair: I don't know his name but I know he is one of the Croydon Road Gang, who live around that area and cause trouble for local shopkeepers and residents. The youth came up to the counter and said, 'Are you going to serve me?' I said, 'No, I've got instructions not to serve any of you.' The youth said, 'I've got nothing to do with that stupid Croydon Road Gang.' I said, 'They are friends of yours. You are always with them. I'm not going to serve you – we don't want any more aggravation from you lot.' At this point Smart came in and produced a knife from his pocket. It was about six inches in length. Smart said, 'You black bastard, I'm going to kill you – you are going to get shot.' I said, 'OK, I've had enough of this aggravation, racial abuse, and threats.' I went to the public part of the shop. Smart ran outside the shop and I saw him kick the large plate-glass window, smashing it. I saw that the customers inside the shop were showered by the flying glass; fortunately, none of them were injured. Smart ran off.[15]

Three weeks later, in another statement to the police, Macauley continued:

On Thursday, 6 November 1986, it all came to a head. I was working in the shop at 257 Barking Road and Mr Lone and his son Naeem Lone came over. I had a chat with Naeem, and Mr Hayat spoke to his father. At about 10.30 p.m. Mr Lone was walking out of the shop into the Barking Road when Jimmy Smart got out of the car, crossed over the road and started shouting abuse like 'Paki', 'you Paki cunt'. Mr Lone went to his car and Smart was still shouting abuse at Mr Lone. Mr Lone was standing there taking all this abuse. Smart shouted to Mr Lone, 'Wait, you wait there,' and then went into Raffles, a public house.

A short time later Smart came out of the pub with his mates: the two youths who were later arrested came out with Smart, Eddie Banstead and several others, whose names I don't know but who I have seen around and can recognize. The group of about fifteen to twenty youths came rushing towards Mr Lone. Smart went up to Mr Lone and started shouting abuse at him and then threw a glass of beer over him, at which point the rest of the group threw their glasses at Mr Lone's car, smashing his side windows. I could see that the group was armed with sticks, steel poles and knives. I saw that Smart had a knife and a stick. I also saw in the crowd a large knife like a kebab knife, about two and a half feet long.

Then they turned on Mr Lone and started to punch, kick, hit him with the sticks. I also saw the knives being used and I heard Mr Lone screaming. I then saw him fall to the ground and the blows continued to rain down on him.

Mr Lone's son Naeem went to help his father and he picked up two bits of wood about a foot long to try and defend himself and his father, who was lying on the ground being beaten. Naeem went into the crowd to help his dad and I saw him hit a few of them. The crowd then turned on Naeem, kicking, punching, hitting him with sticks and knives. I saw Naeem being beaten to the floor like his dad. I heard him screaming. I saw a girl sit on Mr Lone, take her shoe off and hit Mr Lone on the head with her shoe.

This all happened very quickly, so I ran across the road to help Mr Lone and Naeem, since they were both unconscious on the ground. I grabbed hold of Mr Lone and started to pull him away, but Mr Lone couldn't walk or stand and I had to drag him. The group then started hitting me. Smart hit me across the back with a stick, a blond-haired boy hit me over the back with a crutch, and the two youths who were arrested in the pub were also hitting me with sticks. I could see that Mr Lone was bleeding heavily from the face. Once I got Mr Lone clear, I then went back for Naeem and again I got hit with sticks and various things across the back by Smart, the blond-haired boy and the two who were arrested. Naeem was also bleeding from the face: there were bruises to his hands and he was screaming about his arm. Once I had got them clear I saw Smart, the blond-haired youth and the two that were arrested come running after me. I noticed that all of the group of four had knives and sticks. I had to leave Naeem and run to the shop to get something to protect myself. Smart and the others chased me to the shop. I heard Smart shout, 'Get him!' I was frightened for my safety and also for the safety of Naeem and Mr Lone.

I got into the shop and I got hold of a stick, at which point the group saw that I had one and so ran off. The police arrived shortly afterwards and two men who had been involved in the fight were placed in the police vehicle.[16]

Naeem's hand was broken. His father suffered a broken nose, multiple bruises and a slash wound to the face and head; Mubasha needed eight stitches to the face and three to the head.

Newham police do not come well out of the Lone affair. Hayat reports that when he first went to the police after a tip-off that he was about to be attacked, they said they couldn't spare anybody to help and that helping wasn't what they were in Newham to do. Hayat goes on:

They said that if the gang did do anything, we should give the station a call. I said, 'But by that time one of my staff might be seriously hurt. I can't take that chance.'

So I rang for my friends to come round, some West Indian, some Indian. Two minutes after they arrived, two police cars with dogs were outside and, a minute later, a van-full came. The police came in and sent everyone upstairs; then the head of East Ham police station came down with two cars. The police said, 'What are you doing?' I said that my friends were there because their colleagues had said they couldn't help. The police asked what weapons we had, but we had none. They said, 'If you hurt one of them, it'll cause a gang war and we'd have to arrest the whole lot of you.' There were a lot of police around that day.

The next day I saw twenty youths. I rang the police. I said, 'I can't keep calling my friends – can you help?' The police asked if the gang was doing anything yet. I said, 'They are looking threatening.' The police said, 'Only call us if they do anything.' I rang again, for there were more and more youths gathering. I asked the police to send just one person. They said no, that they were too busy. I was to tell them if anything happened. I said I was going to close the shop and asked them to send someone who could prevent us being jumped.

Twenty minutes later a policeman came and told us to hurry up and close.[17]

After Mr Lone and Naeem were beaten up the police did arrest two people: but even this happened only with the assistance of Naeem and Mubasha, who took them into Raffles, the pub, and identified one of the whites who had previously been attacking them by pointing to the blood on the man's clothing as proof.

The man was arrested. Jimmy Smart was also arrested because he was named by the Lones. However, when the case came to court an all-white jury recorded not-guilty verdicts against both culprits. Indeed, when Jimmy Smart and his petrol-bomb attack were discussed one member of the jury inadvertently revealed an interesting device tattooed on his arm: a swastika.

The trials over, Hayat commented: 'After that, I no longer believe that there is any justice in this country. It seems that the only thing you can do is keep your mouth shut and forget about it.'[18]

Later that year Hayat's shop was attacked yet again. Youths were smashing down the door and windows. Mr Hayat was on the phone to the police all the while, but a car took twenty minutes to arrive. Once there, the car's occupants kicked off by questioning Hayat – while his attackers looked on from the other side of the street. The police said they wanted a description of the men. Hayat reports:

I said, 'Look, you can see for yourselves. There they are.' But the police did not arrest anyone, and as soon as they had gone, the youths came back. They began to punch my cousin, calling him a Paki bastard and a 'grass'. The police returned and arrested two men. I was taken to East Ham police station, but the CID interviewed me and accused me of stealing a gold bracelet.[19]

Eventually the youths were brought to trial, and Newham magistrates found them guilty. Mr Hayat was awarded £500 damages – for damage that had cost him £3,000. His shop is now likely to close because of the debts incurred through constant repairs.

Barking Road has dozens of Asian shops and restaurants that are now derelict because of experiences like Ezaz Hayat's. Naeem and Mubasha have now joined a local campaign against racist attacks. It seems likely that many other east London Asians will be forced to follow their example.

Trevor Ferguson

If you are the victim of racial harassment, report the matter immediately to your local police station. Speed is of the essence . . . If the victim of any attack sees a racial motive, it will be given high priority by the police . . . The definition of a racial incident used by the Metropolitan Police is simple: any incident in which it appears to the reporting or investigating officer that the complaint involves an element of racial motivation; or any incident which includes an allegation of racial motivation made by any person.[20]

When they are not suggesting the repulse of petrol-bombs by 'using anything to hand, such as an umbrella or your shoes', the police recommend calling on their services in times of difficulty. As with the Saddiques and the Lones, however, the constabulary's professed concern about racist attacks contrasts vividly with its practical indifference towards them. When, early in 1987, housewife Cherry Reid held a party in Beaconsfield Road, east London, she and her guests found this out to their cost.

Shortly after the party had started, Reid's guests began choking, and some of them vomited. Nobody was quite sure what was happening. Trevor Ferguson, later to be the victim of a brutal assault, arrived late and knocked on the door. He looked through the letterbox and his eyes began to water. Putting one and one together, he surmised that something must have been put through the letterbox to cause the choking and vomiting. Racists had tear-gassed Reid's house. She remembers: 'We called the police immediately and told them to get down to the house. The woman who answered the phone just said, "Sorry, Beaconsfield Road doesn't exist." There I was with a house full of people terrified and in pain and she was telling me the road I lived on didn't exist. Then she hung up.'

After several neighbours had rung the police, they finally turned up at the house. Everybody was sure that the attackers had come from another party across the road, so the police said they would keep watch. Some time later the racists came back with the tear gas. Reid thought the police would get them. When she opened the door the police were nowhere: 'They'd gone.'

Ferguson and Reid's cousin, Gary, had seen two men run across the road and went out to tell them to grow up and pack it in. As they entered the ground floor of the apartment block opposite and climbed the stairs, 'a whole gang of white boys pounced on the two boys, kicking them to the ground. They were shouting, "Kill the niggers, kill the niggers!" They had bottles and smashed one into Trevor's face. His eye almost came out of his head. They smashed bottles on Gary too, and he got slashed on the back of the neck.'

Trevor Ferguson lost the sight of his eye. Reid was stunned by the police reaction to this incident and that of the officers who attended:

The next day, when the police came round, the first thing they said to me was, 'It wasn't a racist attack last night. The other people were just jealous of your party.' I hadn't said it was racist, yet this was the first thing they came out with. There's no doubt in my mind it was racist.

The thing I remember most about the incident was the attitude of the police. They didn't come to help when we first rang. They hung the phone up on us, and when they came round one said, 'I suppose you'll be putting in for a transfer now.' The cheek of it! Suggesting I would use the attack just to get a quick move.

Trevor Ferguson will never use one eye again: it had to be removed under surgery. Despite the fact that the attack took place from a house just over the road from the victims, the police have pressed no charges.

From the experiences of the Saddiques, the Lones and Trevor Ferguson it is clear that Asians and West Indians in Britain can expect only viciousness from white racists among the general public, coupled with casual indifference and cynicism from the police. In Britain black people are second-class citizens. Few institutions are more involved in confirming this status than the police.

2 Institutional harassment

On the whole most blacks are unemployed, like rastafarians who go around with big floppy hats, roller skates and stereo radios, smoking pot and sponging money off the state.[1]

In the wake of initiatives like the Met's pamphlet guide for the racially harassed, many people in Britain have tried to believe that the police have changed their illiberal ways. After all, police forces throughout Britain have made efforts to draw in black recruits – though few have come forward. White policemen have also been sent to language laboratories to learn the dialects of ethnic minorities, and many have been tutored in the sociology of black people in Britain. Several 'bad apple' police officers have been convicted of assaulting blacks. However, racism among the forces of law and order runs extraordinarily deep.

Asked to write essays on black people, cadets at the national police training college, Hendon, recorded the following insights:

All blacks are pains and should be ejected from society.

Wogs, nig-nogs and Pakis . . . come into Britain take up our homes our jobs and our resources and contribute relatively less to our once glorious country. They are, by nature, unintelligent, and can't at all be educated sufficiently to live in a civilized society of the Western world. It is my opinion that they themselves would be better off living in their native lands, so send them packing, carpet bags, funky music, curries, all their relatives and stereo transistor radios.

Questions asked by the cadets included 'Can a twelve-bore shotgun blast a black man into tiny pieces at twelve yards?' and 'Do black people burn better with oil or petrol on them?'[2]

Loathing for blacks is not just a phenomenon among young police cadets. It stretches right to the very top of the force. In June 1982, shortly after he was first appointed to oversee the fight against crime in London, Met Chief Kenneth Newman told a journalist working for the American magazine *Police*: 'In the Jamaicans, you have people who are constitutionally disorderly ... It's simply in their make-up.' Jamaicans were, he said 'constitutionally disposed to be anti-authority'.[3] Five years later Superintendent John Ellis, responsible for the Leeds Chapeltown district, made similarly hostile remarks that were secretly taped by Omprakash Sharma, chair of the Leeds United Asian Organization, during a conversation in which Sharma was complaining about the poor police response to an assault on him. Ellis said: 'There are 15,000 West Indians in this locality, and I can tell you that 15,000 West Indians are very difficult to police. They create all sorts of problems. Drugs is one, prostitution, brothels and vice are others.'[4]. Ellis's remarks were closely followed by similar ones by Bill Ganley, a superintendent responsible for the Harlesden station in north London. He said, 'Ninety-nine per cent of muggers are black.'[5]

If black people are, for the police, congenital deviants, then housing estates lived in by blacks also have inherent defects. In July 1986 the Met announced that estates in the London boroughs of Brent, Southwark, Hackney, Newham, Lambeth, Haringey, Ealing, Hammersmith, Westminster, Lewisham and Greenwich were 'disturbance-prone' and 'high-risk'. Flats in these boroughs were thus marked not only by 'a high density of population and ethnic mix' but also by 'hostility towards police'.[6] Black unruliness, in the view of the police, is built into the very fabric of Britain's inner cities.

It is, however, the deaths and injuries suffered by black people while in police custody that provide the most telling indictment of police racism. To die or to be beaten up at the hands of supposedly impartial enforcers of the law is the ultimate degradation. It also means that if you are attacked by ordinary racists, you think twice before notifying the police. Held in captivity by the police, Clinton McCurbin and Colin Roach learned too late about the kind of treatment that black people can expect from uniformed officers in Britain. Detained in police cells, Trevor Monerville joined a host of other black people who today owe their lives to luck. Let us now turn to racial violence of the 'official' type.

Death in police custody

Clinton McCurbin

Wolverhampton, 20 March 1987. Clinton McCurbin, a 23-year-old unemployed black youth, goes to Next, the fashion chainstore, in Wolverhampton town centre. The manager suspects him of using a stolen credit card and calls the police. A squad car pulls up; two policemen get out. They wrestle McCurbin to the floor and he dies.

At first official spokesmen claim that McCurbin took drugs and so met with a heart attack. Later it is announced that he died of 'asphyxia consistent with restraint during a violent struggle'.[7] At a press conference Superintendent Burton is evasive about the causes of death: 'I would not say it was choking,' he argues. 'I would not say it was strangulation.'[8]

Eye-witnesses saw the treatment of McCurbin differently. One explained: 'The policemen held him face down . . . One had his hand cupped under his chin and was pulling back on his chin, while the other was kneeling on his back. Then he went limp and lifeless.' Another recorded: 'One of the crowd stepped forward and said, "You're killing him. You're killing him," and was told to get out.'[9] McCurbin was left on the floor for more than an hour before an ambulance arrived. Then his corpse was dragged feet-first from the front of the shop into the back, away from public view.

Later West Midlands Chief Constable Geoffrey Dear said that he saw no reason to suspend the officers responsible for the death, PC Michael Hobday, 29, and PC Neil Thomas,

23. Instead the two were granted sick leave so as to recover from their ordeal.[10]

When people in Wolverhampton called for a demonstration to protest against the McCurbin affair, all police leave in West Mercia, Staffordshire, Greater Manchester and Northamptonshire was cancelled. A police spokesman said that extra officers would be drafted into the town 'in anticipation of a large crowd from all over the country' – a crowd that would, he said, 'include a massive nucleus of dissidents who, from our information, are hell-bent on causing violence'.[11] Thus although the demonstration was, in the event, angry but peaceful, the police skilfully swept aside the issue of the violence done to McCurbin, preferring instead to raise fears about the public exercise of democratic rights.

Asked to investigate the McCurbin case by West Midland police, the Police Complaints Authority issued a report in August 1987. It concluded that although McCurbin's death occurred while he was being restrained, it was not a matter for legal or internal police discipline. As a result the Director of Public Prosecutions decided that no charges should be preferred. Today McCurbin is dead and buried – as far as the police are concerned. Wolverhampton's black community is angry: its members know that some policemen may now think they have *carte blanche* to kill and get away with it.

On 31 January 1988, almost a year after his killing, the inquest into the death of Clinton McCurbin opened. Legal advisers won a delay so that a high court could consider the right of the family to veto jurors in order to get a mixed jury. In an area with a large black population not one of the eleven originally asked to attend was black.[12]

Colin Roach

Stoke Newington, north London, 12 January 1983. Shortly after his release from a twenty-one day jail sentence in Pentonville prison Colin Roach, a young unemployed black man not long out of school, is found in the foyer of Stoke Newington police station with gunshot wounds in his head and a sawn-off shotgun nearby. Roach, the police say, used the gun to commit suicide; at the subsequent inquest a jury endorses this view. And yet . . .

The gun had no fingerprints or blood on it. The police argued that Roach had carried it into and out of their premises – but the bag they held up as evidence was too small to contain it. The police also told the national press that Roach had a history of mental illness, but this claim too has been proven to be untrue.

Roach died at 11.35 p.m. His father, James, arrived at the station an hour later. At 1.50 a.m. the police issued a press statement on the death – as in the case of Clinton McCurbin, *before* a proper autopsy had been conducted. Only at 3 a.m. however, did the police bother to inform James Roach of the fate of his son.

Colin Roach's death provoked huge demonstrations. More than eighty people were arrested, including James Roach. The *Economist* could make 'neither head nor tail' of Roach's last hours.[13] But two previous incidents connected with Stoke Newington police station suggest that its notoriety is well deserved.

In 1971 Aseta Simms, a black woman, died at the station. Police said that she fell and hit her head, but to this day her family is unconvinced. Although there was conclusive medical evidence that Simms was the victim of repeated blows administered to her skull, the coroner, Douglas Chambers, returned a verdict of 'death by misadventure'. Twelve years later the same coroner dealt with the inquest of Colin Roach – and once again the police were exonerated.

Not quite dead in police custody

Trevor Monerville[14]

In January 1987 PC Macarthy, stationed also at Stoke Newington police station, was found guilty of forcing a Nigerian woman, Adebola Makenjuola, to have sex with him. He told her that she was an illegal immigrant but that, for sexual favours, he would ensure that she could remain in Britain.[15]

While Makenjuola has recovered from her ordeal, Trevor Monerville, a 19-year-old West Indian boy, has not. Having spent three days in the custody of Stoke Newington police, the physical and mental damage he has suffered will be with him for life. As Trevor's father, John, puts it, 'Trevor's past I will not talk about, simply because I've got to accept Trevor as he is now, but I cannot get the old Trevor back, so I will not discuss the old Trevor.'[16]

The Monervilles live in Hackney and Stoke Newington. John runs a television and hi-fi repair shop, and his brother, three sisters and parents all live locally. Before he received his injuries Trevor was training to take part in John's business. Then, on New Year's Eve 1986, Trevor went out on the town with two of his aunts, Carol and Cassy.

After a few drinks the three made their way to a nightclub in Stoke Newington's Church Street. On arrival, Trevor, a shy individual not given to frequent partying, decided not to go in. Because one of his two aunts was already ensconced, however, the other went in to retrieve her so that they could all go home. Five minutes later the two women came out to find that Trevor had vanished. Worried, they went to a nearby mini-cab office to see if he had taken a taxi – but he hadn't. It was not like Trevor just to go off. By now it was after 1.30 a.m. on New Year's Day. Carol and Cassy went home to telephone the rest of the family to find out if Trevor was with any of them. Again they had no luck.

Later that morning Trevor was still at neither his father's house nor his grandparents'. His father became increasingly concerned. By the afternoon the family had decided to go to Stoke Newington police, only to be told that they would have to come back the following day if they wanted to file a missing person report.

On Friday, 2 January 1987, at about 4 p.m., John and Carol returned with a photograph of Trevor. Asked if the young man was in the cells, the police duty officer replied that he was not and duly filed a missing person report. Yet Trevor Monerville *was* in police custody. He had been locked up for at least sixteen hours before his family's visit – a fact that the police were later forced to admit.

John and Carol were distraught. John spent all Friday night and the following day looking for Trevor but to no avail. Then on Sunday, after spending hours telephoning all London's police stations and prisons, John at last learned of Trevor's whereabouts. Monerville was in the hospital wing of Brixton prison. At no point had the police notified his family that he was in their custody. Only because of their persistence did the family find the boy.

On Monday, 5 January, John Monerville and his brother-in-law, Larry, visited Trevor in Brixton prison. John, in a legal statement following his visit, takes up the tale:

I was asked by a senior officer, named Brown, whether there had ever been any epilepsy in my family. I asked him why. He replied that my son had had three epileptic fits and that he had had to wash him twice today, since he had been shitting and urinating in bed. I was told that I should not expect too much when I see him.

Quite understandably, John Monerville was deeply upset by these remarks and feared that Trevor had suffered some terrible accident. He was then taken to see Trevor.

I was profoundly shocked upon seeing my son after five days and seeing the injuries he had sustained during this time. On touching his head, which was extremely sore and covered with bumps, making him jump back in pain, I also noticed a severely blackened, puffed-up and perforated left eye. His right eye was fixed in an abnormal position and could not focus on me whilst I was talking to him. The inside of his mouth was perforated and covered in blood, and his jaw was swinging to the right. His left shoulder and the back of his head was heavily bruised. His chest was heavily bruised also, and his ribs, especially on the left hand side of his body, showed signs of severe bruising.

This bruising also extended to his thighs and buttocks. From his knees to his feet, his legs were covered in congealed blood and scabs. His feet, above and below, were covered in round bruising marks. He told me he had severe pains all over his body and acute headache and abdominal pains. His hair was covered in dry vomit, and his overall condition was extremely distressing for him and to me.

In this condition Trevor Monerville was laid out on a mattress on the prison floor, totally naked. He had been there since Saturday, 3 January 1987, except for a brief visit to King's College Hospital, where he had had a brain scan.

On Thursday, 8 January, Monerville underwent emergency surgery at the Maudsley Hospital in south London. A blood clot and swelling on the brain were treated, but the whole left side of his body remained paralysed. Doctors remarked that Trevor appeared to have been dealt a blow or blows to the head. Today he is unlikely ever to recover fully. Even now he cannot remember what happened to him. All there is to go on is a series of facts gleaned from police records. Monerville's whereabouts between 1.30 a.m. and 10.40 p.m. on New Year's Day 1987 are still a mystery.

Police admit to arresting Monerville at 10.40 p.m. after a motorist, whom they describe as 'a member of the public', found Trevor sleeping on the back seat of his car on the Kingsgate Estate, near Dalston in east London. The car had a broken front offside window, and Monerville was arrested for criminal damage. Strangely, police claim that Monerville was sleeping so deeply when apprehended that he could not be roused throughout the thirty-four hours that he spent in Stoke Newington police station.

Monerville was visited by police surgeons five times and was taken to Homerton Hospital twice. On his last medical inspection, which was held at 1.45 a.m. on 3 January, a police doctor said that he would need a brain scan if his condition did not improve by daylight. His condition did not improve – but no scan was done. Instead he was taken to Highbury magistrates' court, where he was charged with criminal damage. Too poorly to go into court, Monerville was remanded in custody by a magistrate who saw him in his cell. Since he was unconscious, he could ask for no legal advice. He never knew he had been charged or remanded. Then he was taken from the court, by police, to Brixton prison.

There are three other relevant pieces of information. First, on 2 January Monerville was forcibly fingerprinted by six officers at 8.06 p.m. – one minute after being told, while still unconscious, that he was to be detained for failure to give his home address. According to police records, the whole exercise took all of five minutes. One hour later a police doctor remarked that Monerville had a discoloured left eyelid and that his right pupil was dilated and sluggish. He advised that the patient was not in a fit condition to be detained and that he should instead go to hospital.

Second, prison officials destroyed some of Monerville's clothing after his arrival at Brixton. This was done without his permission or that of his family or their legal advisers.

Finally, as soon as Monerville's circumstances in Brixton emerged, Stoke Newington police issued a statement saying that he had a brain tumour. This was not true. It is still unclear why the statement was made.

Police dropped all charges against Monerville on 8 January 1987, reputedly for humanitarian reasons. But they still need to answer the following questions.

1. Did Monerville have bruises and cuts over the length of his body when the police found him? If so, why was he denied hospitalization and instead charged with an offence? If not, which policeman inflicted these injuries on him later? Either way, why were these injuries not discovered during the five visits that Monerville received from five police doctors or during the two that he made to Homerton Hospital?

2. Why did it take six officers five minutes to fingerprint an unconscious man? Why, immediately after this fingerprinting, was it necessary for Monerville to see three doctors within six hours? What happened to cause this?

3. Why did police not inform the Monerville family that they were holding Trevor?

4. Why did prison officers destroy some of Monerville's clothes?

5. Why did the police invent a brain tumour for the man?

6. Why did the police suddenly drop all charges against him?

On 31 March 1987 Stoke Newington police circulated, to local community groups, a letter signed by Inspector Terence Walters. It was directed against what by then had become the Friends and Family of Trevor Monerville Campaign. The letter stated that Monerville's family had 'sinister' motives. One passage was remarkable for its hypocrisy:

A campaign is currently being waged in Hackney concerning a young man who, after being in police and prison custody, underwent an operation at Maudsley Hospital. The innuendo being that his injuries were caused as a result of his treatment by police. Such innuendo is totally presumptuous at this stage. We are more anxious than anyone that this matter be properly investigated.[17]

Chief Superintendent John Peck of Stoke Newington police made a similar point when interviewed in the *Voice* on 1 April 1987. Conceding that the failure to tell John Monerville of his son's whereabouts was a 'mistake' and one that deserved an apology, he added, 'This situation is being manipulated by political agitators.'

During June 1987 Stoke Newington police station was closed down so that a new building could be erected on its site. Officers were dispersed to other stations in the Hackney area.

In the spring of 1987 junior Health Minister Edwina Currie called a public inquiry into Monerville's stay in hospital. But what the Monervilles want to know is: who inflicted the injuries the boy received? The Police Complaints Authority is supposed to be investigating this, but, thirteen months after Monerville became paralysed it has still to make a report – despite claims that it clears up complaints within thirty-seven days.[18]

General harassment by the police

There is in our inner cities a very large minority of people who are not fit for salvage . . . The only way in which the police can protect society is quite simply by harassing these people and frightening them so they are afraid to commit crimes.[19]

There are two conflicting demands. One is to stop harassing young blacks in the inner cities. The other is to stop young blacks harassing other people in the inner cities. Which demand do you respond to? It has to be the second.[20]

1. Are you visible after sunset?
2. Hobbies: mugging, prostitution, pimping (tick as applicable).
3. Please tick your diet: curry, pet food, potatoes.
4. Asians only: when and where did you illegally enter Britain?
5. Asians only: are you toilet-trained?
6. Name of father if known (West Indians should list all possibilities on a separate sheet).
7. Father's occupation: peat cutter, bus conductor, lavatory cleaner, underground guard.[21]

These public, premeditated comments by police officers and the extract from a 'jocular' Middlesbrough police question-naire reveal that the police do more than simply lash out at black people. They act against blacks not only violently and on impulse but also in a lower-key yet more sustained, fashion. The case of Russell Christie, as well as those of a succession of black recruits to the police force, show the pattern all too clearly.

Russell Christie[22]

Russell Christie is a driver/labourer working for the London borough of Hammersmith. Until a few years ago his next-door neighbour was Roger Turner, a special constable at Shepherds Bush station. In May 1985 Christie was charged with threatening to kill Turner following an altercation be-tween them outside their homes. He spent more than six months remanded in custody before being acquitted, in a trial that lasted no more than ten minutes, in November 1985. During his detention his girlfriend suffered a miscarriage. Turner moved house when Christie was let out of prison, and for some time the two didn't meet – except for a brief encounter when Turner joked about Christie's incarceration and his girlfriend's miscarriage.

The story from then on is a disturbing case of racist victimization by police officers. The quotations below are all taken from court records relating to Russell Christie's case. They were made available to me by John Fitzpatrick and Beverley Brown, the lawyers representing Christie at his trial.

On 28 January 1987 Christie and a friend named Smiler pulled into a local garage for petrol. Christie was in the queue to pay when he heard a menacing voice from behind. He looked round, saw Turner and told him to leave him alone. An argument ensued. Turner said to Christie, 'I'll get you seven years this time.'

On 12 February Turner put his words into action. Christie was arrested and charged with making a threat to kill, under a law that dated back to 1861. Turner argued that Christie had spat at him and had said, 'I'm going to kill you.' Christie was again remanded in custody. He applied for bail three times, but all applications were refused, and Christie found himself in prison, awaiting trial, for more than three months.

It materialized later that police from Shepherds Bush station had, a day before Christie's application for bail, interviewed Suresh Majithia, the owner of the garage in which the exchange between Christie and Turner had taken place. In the interview Majithia had contested Turner's version of events, saying that there had been no spitting and no threats to kill on his premises. Majithia had also stated that Smiler had proposed to Christie that he avoid a confrontation and that Christie had seemed keen to do just that. However Majithia's statement was not released by the police either to Christie's bail judges or to the defence until vigorous protests had been made. If it had been released properly, it is unlikely that Christie would have remained in custody.

After a two-day trial held at Knightsbridge Crown Court in May 1987, a jury concluded unanimously that Christie was not guilty. Indeed, the trial judge said that he had never heard of such a case before, demanded to know why it had been brought and asked for an inquiry into the police station that had brought it – Shepherds Bush. After months behind bars, Christie may seek damages from the police for malicious prosecution. One of the factors behind Christie's eventual acquittal was the defence made on his behalf by John Fitzpatrick, a Hammersmith solicitor and a member of War Against Racism (WAR). Fitzpatrick told me that the Christies had suffered police harassment before.[23]

Victor Ranger

On 22 February 1987 Victor Ranger, a black man from Handsworth, Birmingham, made the mistake of parking his BMW on the zig-zag lines marking a zebra crossing. Approached by a police officer, he was asked where he had stolen the car he had been driving. When he replied that he had bought it himself, the police officer was reported to have said, 'Where did you get the money to buy a car like this from – pushing drugs?'

Ranger was then asked to produce a driving licence on the spot. He could not, so the police officer followed him home to Hampstead Road, in the Lozells area of Birmingham, where his licence was. Realizing, as he emerged from his house with papers in hand, that he had picked up the wrong documents, he turned to go back for the correct ones. Within minutes no fewer than fourteen police cars arrived on the scene.

There were three other people in the house: Ranger's girlfriend Maeve, her daughter Peggy and Maeve's 70-year-old mother. They came out to see what was happening and tried to stop it. The old lady claims to have been knocked to the ground and told that she would be arrested for obstruction if she didn't get back inside. She was eventually taken to hospital. Ranger was finally arrested and charged with having a faulty licence, damaging a police helmet and possessing an offensive weapon.

Ranger's case didn't come to court until September 1987, after more than six months of uncertainty had elapsed. By that time only the charge relating to the driving licence remained. The police alleged that Ranger had had two driving licences and that, when they had apprehended him, he had tried to tear up one that was 'a strange colour and typed with a manual typewriter, not a computer'. They alleged that he had then passed this licence to Maeve and that she had disappeared inside the house with it. This was odd, given that Maeve says that, like her mother, she had been knocked to the ground at the time. As for the bogus licence, this has never been seen.

The police, confronted with a weak case, went to the trouble of doing a great deal of investigation into Ranger's background. Eventually they came up with the following additional charges:

1. Obtaining pecuniary advantage by deception when insuring the BMW in 1979.
2. Abusing the 1972 Traffic Act by parking on a zig-zag line.
3. Assault on a police officer with actual bodily harm – namely, a thumb so badly sprained that the officer had to take a whole day off work.
4. Assault on a police officer while resisting arrest – namely, a kick in the back of the leg.

The magistrate considering the case found Ranger guilty on all five counts, gave him two suspended three-month prison sentences and fined him £350. When sentencing him the magistrate observed that the court had been 'used' by him 'to weave an intricate web of lies about racial harassment'. He then authorized an investigation into Ranger's income. Finally he said of Ranger, 'If he can run a car, he can pay costs.'[24]

Black police recruits: Booth, Edwards, Lall

In the face of cases like that of Russell Christie, it is not surprising that police campaigns to recruit black people to the force have largely failed. However, that has not prevented a nearly all-white force from harassing black recruits.

Nicholas Orlando Booth joined West Yorkshire police as a probationary constable in April 1985. *The Times* reported that on training courses he found himself called a 'black bastard' and 'nigger'.[25] He was rapidly disillusioned and left the force.

Once a South London policeman, Mark Edwards left the force after meeting with experiences similar to Booth's. Since his resignation Edwards has found himself charged with minor offences on no fewer than six occasions, only to be acquitted each time. Edwards, who now works in a South London pharmacy is rueful:

I have experienced police racism from the inside. I've been persist-ently hounded since deciding to leave. Even when I was in the force they used me like a pet animal – wheeling me out, together with the mascot, every time TV cameras were looking for a story. I can see no possibility of black people getting a fair deal from the kind of people I came across in the force. Before I didn't believe a lot of the stuff about police racism and so on, now I know it is all too true.[26]

Asian police officer Krishnand Lall had the misfortune to take a holiday with white police colleagues. As reported in the *Sun*, he was called a 'bloody Paki' and clubbed with bottles by his fellow officers. As a result, his ear was partly severed and he spent four days in hospital.[27]

Even when they are in numbered blue uniforms, black people can expect a special kind of handling from the forces of law and order. Reassuring leaflets, language lessons and ethnic recruitment are unlikely to change the distrust in which police are held by black people. The kind of handling they receive from the police is what sparks the periodic upris-ings Britain has seen in its inner cities.

Broadwater Farm

Violence from neighbours, intimidation by supervisors, violence and general harassment on the part of the police: black people know what to expect in modern Britain. On Broadwater Farm, Tottenham, London, hundreds of West Indians made this discovery. Accompanied by a media panic directed against black lawlessness, the Farm affair stands as a symbol of what blacks in Britain can look forward to in the 1990s.

In March 1987 three young men were sentenced to life imprisonment, convicted of the murder of P C Keith Blakelock. Winston Silcott, Mark Braithwaite and Engin Raghip have since begun their thirty-year terms in Wormwood Scrubs prison. The convictions were secured after a trial that was the subject of intense media interest. A few publications, notably the *Guardian* and the *New Statesman*, expressed some concern over the judicial procedure used to gain convictions. That there was no wider outcry over the fate of the three men, however, was a salient feature of their case. On the contrary, the overwhelming majority of Britain's printed and broadcast media succeeded in persuading the population that, even if the three men were not responsible for Blakelock's death, they were guilty by association and thus deserved everything they got. Apart from various anti-racist organizations, only Amnesty International, in its February 1988 report on the Broadwater Farm prisoners, has stood out and described the three imprisoned for murder, and the many others locked up for minor offences, as political prisoners.[28]

Clearly, the events at Broadwater Farm, in which a black mother and a white policeman died in the space of forty-eight hours, were horrifying for those directly or indirectly involved. The killing of Blakelock gripped the mind of the public, and that of Mrs Cynthia Jarrett, coming as it did a week after the shooting of Cherry Groce in Brixton, spread fear among Britain's black community. The sense of outrage at Blakelock's murder, exacerbated by media treatment of the events, has, I am convinced, denied a fair trial to the three youths and also allowed the police to gain convictions by the use of methods of investigation that included hearsay and rumour. The near-unanimous acceptance of the outcome of the trial makes countering the jury's verdict a lonely enterprise. Yet there was, quite literally, nothing in the evidence presented to justify the convictions.

The events surrounding the eruption of Broadwater Farm on 6 October 1985, and the eventual verdict on the three defendants, need inspecting in some detail in order to sustain these claims. It is our belief that, if the verdicts remain unchallenged, then the methods used at Broadwater Farm will soon become commonplace, and a further erosion of democratic rights in Britain will take place.

The saga begins at about 1 p.m. on Saturday 5 October 1985, when Floyd Jarrett, a young man of West Indian parentage, was driving his BMW along Roseberry Avenue in Tottenham. He came across a familiar situation when he was stopped by police and asked whether he owned the car he was driving. This kind of random car stop is often carried out on black youth in the inner cities.

One of the three officers accosting Jarrett, PC Allen, filled out a form requiring him to take his driving documents to the police station. Another, PC Casey, contacted the Police National Computer to check up on the car – a step rarely taken over minor car offences but all too often made when those suspected of them are black. (Later, after the case came up in the magistrates' court, counsel for Jarrett's defence asked PC Casey whether a National Computer check would have been carried out had he, Jarrett's white solicitor, been stopped; the answer was no. Casey could give no reason for his actions other than that Jarrett was black and driving an expensive car.)[29]

Although Casey's check showed that car and occupant were in order, Jarrett was arrested for the theft of a motor vehicle. Alarmed, he ran across the road. The arresting officers claimed that he aimed two blows in their direction, one of which hit Casey in the face. An independent witness, an architect, later testified in court that no punches were thrown. Nevertheless, Jarrett was charged with assault, only to be acquitted when brought to court in December 1985. On this occasion the presiding magistrate insisted that costs amounting to £350 be awarded against the police. As for the charge of theft, this had to be dropped.

By 3.30 p.m. that day, however, Tottenham police had established Jarrett's identity, charged him and put him in a cell. A little more than one hour later Detective Constable Michael Randall, an off-duty CID officer doing paperwork at Tottenham station, visited Jarrett and, as the station's custody record notes, recognized him. Randall concluded that the prisoner's home should be searched, persuaded the duty officer, Inspector Clarke, to go about this and determined to go on the search himself – despite being off duty.[30]

For a house search to be made after an arrest for a motoring offence and an assault is, again, most peculiar. The conduct of the search itself revealed that the officers making it were unsure what they were looking for. Randall claimed to have detailed information to the effect that Jarrett was guilty of handling stolen goods, yet neither the source for this information, nor any evidence that it was true, has ever come to light.

The space on the search warrant where police normally enter what they are looking for contained the legend 'diverse goods'. The search was amateurish, suggesting that the police knew that they would find no stolen goods: indeed, told that a locked room in the Jarrett house was left unchecked, a coroner later described the search as 'the most ridiculous thing I have ever heard'.[31]

It is unlikely that the officers had a proper search warrant when they visited the Jarrett household. It may have been issued after the search but not before it. Inspector Clarke says that the warrant was signed at 5 p.m.: DC Randall claims that it was issued by the magistrate at 5.15 p.m. The magistrate himself gave three differing times: he told later investigators from Essex police that he had signed the warrant at 6.30 p.m. – well after the search of the Jarrett house; he told an inquest that he had signed it at 5.45 p.m.; finally, in a second interview with Essex police, he explained that he had signed the warrant between 5.30 and 6.15 p.m. In the police record of the outcome of the search D C Randall failed to fill out the part of the form asking for the name of the magistrate agreeing to the operation. When it was later put to him that this was because no warrant authorizing the search had been obtained in the first place, he replied, 'I can't remember why I missed it out.'[32] Patricia Jarrett, Jarrett's sister, claims that, although it was requested, no warrant was ever shown to her.

The course of events during this search has since become clear. Four police officers arrived at the Jarrett home at about 5.45 p.m.: D C Randall, Sergeant Parsons, P C Casey and P C Allan. Although off duty, D C Randall took charge. The house was entered not by knocking and being admitted [33] but by means of Jarrett's keys, which D C Randall took from the police station without signing them out with the duty officer, Sergeant Bowell.

Mrs Cynthia Jarrett, her daughter Patricia, a 2-year-old child, and Jerome, her grandson, were all in the house. They were extremely shocked when they discovered police officers walking into their home, and they knew that Sergeant Parsons was lying when he told them that their front door had been open. After searching the upstairs bedrooms, D C Randall moved towards the dining room. Mrs Jarrett was in the doorway. Patricia Jarrett takes up the story:

D C Randall went into the dining room. My mother had put Jerome into the armchair and was standing in the doorway. He took his left arm, pushed her out of the way. She fell with one arm in the armchair and the rest of her body towards the armchair . . . I tried to help her up. She was gasping for breath and gasping quite heavily.[34]

Cynthia had had a serious fall – one that had broken a small table. Patricia telephoned for an ambulance and was told that

one was on its way. D C Randall paid no attention throughout: instead, he scrutinized the Jarretts' hi-fi and television
and the contents of a number of chests of drawers.

At this point Michael Jarrett, Floyd's brother, came in. He
asked an officer if he had a warrant but received no reply.
Meanwhile D C Randall embarked on a visit to the loft. By
now Cynthia was breathing hard. Then Patricia recounts:

> She tumbled sidewards out of the dining room chair, lying on her
> side. I rushed over and started talking to her . . . I put my ear to her
> mouth to see if I could feel any breath. I felt for her pulse but did
> not feel any pulse. I blocked her nose, opened her mouth and gave
> mouth to mouth resuscitation. Nothing was happening. She looked
> up at me, her eyes keeled over, her head slumped back and she was
> completely still. I ran from the house screaming into the street.[35]

The ambulance arrived at 6.11 p.m. Mrs Jarrett was pronounced dead on arrival at North Middlesex Hospital at 6.35
p.m.

At the subsequent inquest the police tried to blame Mrs
Jarrett's death on the excitable behaviour of her daughter.
But the police themselves did not find Patricia Jarrett troub-
lesome, for at 5.55 p.m. D C Randall radioed Tottenham
station with the message that there were 'no problems'. There
were no problems – except that Mrs Jarrett was already on
the floor and an ambulance had already been called.

Mrs Jarrett had high blood pressure and heart disease. But
it was police action that prompted her death. At the inquest
the jury acknowledged this by refusing to pass a verdict of
death by natural causes. Unable to conclude that D C Randall
had purposely caused her death, it recorded a verdict of ac-
cidental death.

In summary: police stopped Floyd Jarrett and went beyond
normal procedure in checking up on his car; they charged
him with an assault of which he was later acquitted; they
entered his house using his keys; they searched his home;
and they pushed Mrs Jarrett over and, during her last minutes of consciousness, continued with their search. Later the

Police Complaints Authority found that the police officers had done nothing wrong. It was agreed that no criminal or disciplinary charges should be made against them.

Floyd Jarrett was released at 7 p.m. The police didn't bother to tell him that his mother was dead, but they did try to explain things to the media. On the following day the *Mail on Sunday* dutifully reported that, according to Scotland Yard, Cynthia 'became ill after she was in a struggle with officers who visited her home following the arrest of her son'.[36]

As a result of the extensive media coverage of Mrs Jarrett's death, everybody on her estate knew about it within twenty-four hours. Speaking at an inquiry into the disturbances, Stafford Scott, a member of the Broadwater Farm Youth Association, described the feeling:

Because it has happened before – police officers have taken away people's keys and entered their homes without alerting the people inside – it was easy for people to believe it had happened in this instance. Because people have seen police manhandling members of their families whilst raiding, it was easy to believe in this instance. So what was actually taking place was a lot of emotional transferral. They weren't just thinking, 'Floyd Jarrett's mother died today'; they were thinking in terms that it could very easily have been their mother. So people were feeling very sickened by what had happened. People were very upset.[37]

As is typical in inner-city 'hot spots', the police responded by implementing both a 'soft' and a 'hard' strategy simultaneously. They organized a meeting for local community leaders and the Jarrett family, and they sent in reinforcements.

At the meeting Deputy Assistant Commissioner Richards spoke from the chair and said that he and his men could neither discuss the case nor suspend the officers involved, since the whole matter had been placed in the hands of the Police Complaints Authority. But this was untrue. The Police Complaints Authority is a formally independent body that when requested, asks the officers of one force to investigate a complaint against another. The Authority has no power to make issues *sub judice*; neither does it have the power to suspend internal police disciplinary procedures.

Told that the police would not discuss the case, a meeting of the Broadwater Farm Youth Association later resolved to picket Tottenham police station to indicate its anger – an emotion that ran so deep that even Bernie Grant, a left-wing Labour man and leader of the local council, was not allowed to address the meeting. Stafford Scott's mother later described her plea for calm at the meeting: 'I shouted at them and asked them to listen to what Bernie had to say. But they thought Bernie was more white-minded. That was the opinion of most of them, that Bernie wasn't going to give them their rights.'[38] At 6.45 p.m. the meeting broke up. People began to move off in small groups towards the police station.

By this time the police had drafted 200 extra officers into the area. As black youths leaving for the police station neared the edge of the estate, three transit vans packed with officers in full riot gear drove into the Farm. They were greeted by a rain of blows on their doors and sides. Within minutes, riot squads had surrounded the estate, refusing to let people leave. From this point on local people began to barricade the entrances to the estate and to prevent the police from coming in. *New Society* reporter Steven Platt records the atmosphere:

A black couple trying to leave the area via Willan Road were turned back at the police lines, to a chorus of the monkey noises used to abuse black footballers by racists at football matches. 'Fuck off, niggers,' yelled one of the policemen. 'Go and live in a zoo' . . . 'Get back in your rat hole, vermin,' echoed another, 'we'll be in to get you soon enough.'[39]

The independent inquiry into the Broadwater Farm events, conducted by Lord Gifford, estimated that perhaps 2,000 police were deployed on the estate. Peter Grey, a local eye-witness, describes events:

When I first heard about Cynthia Jarrett I was watching

television and everyone went quiet. We thought it was really bad. I mean – what had she done to anybody? She was just a black woman. Later I was going past on a bus when I saw this fire and I jumped off to have a look. This was at about seven o'clock. There were loads of police. Youths were throwing bricks and bottles at the police, but the police were giving as good as they got. They were throwing the stuff back, and every now and then they'd rush into the crowd and grab someone – not to arrest them, but to give them a good hiding . . .[40]

In the course of these events a group of police officers, including P C Keith Blakelock, were sent into the estate and became separated from their colleagues. Isolated, they were set upon by a number of angry tenants; P C Blakelock was stabbed and died instantly. The following day the papers were full of accounts of bloodthirsty 'black mobs butchering an innocent policeman'. The gruesome details of Blakelock's murder were scattered across the tabloid press.

As in most cases of violent conflict, there were, no doubt, some individuals who relished the situation. But the street fighting in Tottenham stemmed not from a mad bloodlust but rather from the sense of outrage most tenants now felt towards the police. Mrs Jarrett died following an unorthodox police entry into her home. Blakelock was murdered. After that, further police sorties began.

Once the situation had calmed down, in the early hours of 6 October 1985, Broadwater Farm was occupied by perhaps as many as 300 police. They were seen entering in large numbers at about 4.30 a.m. George Martin, a community leader and a member of the West Indian Leadership Council, describes the invasion:

I was standing at the door of the Youth Association, and we saw the police as they came upstairs, and they went towards the supermarket, and I saw one of them hitting something. I was trying to see, but it was in darkness. He had a shield and he had a baton. He was hitting this thing, down like this. Eventually when I managed to look, he picked this thing up and chained it against the door. Then I realized it was a young chap.[41]

The door to the Youth Association was smashed by truncheons. The officers came equipped with plastic bullets. One youth was taken out and systematically beaten. The officers then spread out and occupied the entire estate.[42]

Mrs Jarrett's fate was submerged by media dominated by Blakelock's death and the use, during civil unrest, of firearms against the police for the first time in mainland Britain. Public outrage supported the ensuing police campaign on Broadwater Farm. Between 7 October and 16 December 1985 the independent inquiry found that the following numbers of police were deployed:

7 October	1,409
8,9 October	3,732
10–14 October	9,165
15–18 October	3,044
19–20 October	3,044
21–27 October	3,213
28 October – 4 November	3,744
5–11 November	3,744
12–18 November	3,104
19–25 November	1,736
26 November – 2 December	1,715
3–9 December	1,715
10–16 December	1,051

Between 10 October 1985 and May 1986 police searched 271 homes, broke down eighteen doors with sledge-hammers, arrested 362 people, charged 167 people with offences relating to the events of 6 October 1985 and held no fewer than six for Blakelock's murder. More than 70 per cent of those arrested were black on an estate in which nearly half the inhabitants were white. Mrs Scott's experience is instructive:

While I was ironing I heard the gate open and two persons talk, so I thought somebody was coming to the door. I looked, but I didn't see anybody. Then I saw someone rush across the window, and I saw one officer pointing a gun up. I went over to look and I saw one pointing to my bedroom, one at the gate with his hand on the trigger, pointing straight at the front door and one next door pointing like this. I heard my daughter scream, the youngest one. She was partly dressed in the bathroom, and there were three pointing guns at her . . . Others surrounded the place.[43]

Seven armed police entered Mrs Scott's home with weapons, saying they were searching for guns. They took food, clothes, photographs and personal belongings. Mrs Scott's son, Stafford, was arrested the same day. He was detained for thirty-six hours without charge.

The 362 arrested were taken to fourteen police stations, where many of them were held without access to their families or to legal advice. Tottenham police station was never used. The police were apparently intent on interrogating suspects without interruption and for long periods. A total of 167 people were charged, while 195 were released with no charge. Of those charged the largest number – seventy – were charged with affray. Three were charged with riot, twenty with threatening behaviour, one with making petrol bombs, twelve with possessing petrol bombs, thirteen with possessing stolen goods, eight with having an offensive weapon, seven with theft, four with obstruction, four with arson and three with assault on police. The remainder were charged with offences not directly associated with the events of 6 October.

Of the above cases sixty-eight were heard at the Old Bailey. There nineteen people pleaded guilty and forty-nine not guilty. Of those pleading not guilty the majority, twenty-six were cleared. This was not too surprising, given that no fewer than thirty-seven of those claiming their innocence were charged on the basis of confessions alone.[44] Nearly all of these confessions were disputed in court; those signing them claimed that they had been made under duress.

Up to a hundred people were held for two, and sometimes

three, days without charge. Many of them suffered further detention for up to seventy-two hours at the instruction of local magistrates.

The case of Howard Kerr is revealing. Kerr, 17 years old, was detained for sixty hours, during which he told police that, on the night of 6 October 1985, he had been in Windsor. Later, however, he confessed to taking part in the events, named twenty others who had done the same, referred to the existence on the estate of a 'factory' for making petrol bombs and described what he had seen happen to PC Blakelock. Kerr's statement ran to fifty typed pages. But it later became clear, through independent witnesses, that he had indeed been in Windsor at the critical moment and could not have seen any of the things he had described. Kerr told us that, while in custody, he had been so frightened that he had conveyed to his tormentors anything they wanted to hear. This pattern is central to the case of the three men accused of murdering PC Blakelock.

Peter Grey's experience is also relevant here. Grey told us:

When I was in the police cell they beat me up. They came into the cell in the morning and beat me up. Then they came back in the afternoon and beat me up again, just kicking and punching and pushing me around.

Then they took me upstairs, told me to stand against a wall and asked me what I had in my top pocket. Before I could answer, this policeman punched me in the stomach, then elbowed me and walked away. Then he turned around, elbowed me in the chest, grabbed hold of my head, shoved it against a table and then rubbed it into a table. He said that if I didn't answer their questions, they were going to hit me some more.[45]

Peter Grey is black. Police claimed that a black man, looking like Mr T. from the television series *The A Team*, had organized the fighting at Broadwater Farm and had killed PC Blakelock with a machete. Although Grey looks nothing like Mr T., he was arrested for murder while in the public gallery at Tottenham magistrates' court during the trial of a friend.

Held for three days at Wood Green police station, he confessed to participating in the fighting and was eventually released on curfew.

Grey finally appeared at the Old Bailey. He was locked up between every session of the court, and allowed access to his barrister only once. Yet he won his case. His barber testified that he had never had a Mr T. haircut, and, after police witnesses gave conflicting and confused stories, the jury threw out the case against him.

The quotations that follow are all taken from records of the trial of the man charged with Blakelock's killing.

Mark Pennant was the first of six youths to be arrested for murder. Fifteen years old, he was held for three days, questioned six times for a total of ten hours and, at one stage, put in a cell on his own for four hours. When Pennant's solicitor arrived at the police station, police turned him away.

In his statement Pennant claimed to have been 5 yards from the spot where Blakelock had fallen. He said he had kicked and cut Blakelock before wiping his knife and giving it to somebody else. He also claimed to have made petrol bombs, and he named others who had hit Blakelock.

All of this may have seemed convincing but for one snag: Pennant was severely retarded. He could not read, do figures or remember very much at all. He had been under duress. Dismissing the case against him, the judge, Justice Hodgson, argued, 'Four hours of isolation, for a boy of 15 with a mental age of 7, who should not have been in a cell at all, is oppression.' The judge also pointed out that the manner of the arrest of Pennant was illegal, that holding him in a cell was a violation of the Young Persons Act 1969 and that denying him a solicitor, access to his parents and details of the allegations against him were all irregular.

Jason Hill, 13 years old and the only white defendant, was held for four days and interrogated five times for a total of fifteen hours. He first claimed that he had only watched the men surrounding Blakelock's body, but, under further questioning, he admitted to cutting Blakelock with a sword. After being taken to court and seeing a solicitor, he immediately retracted his statements, saying that the police had pressurized him to give the account he had and contending that he had not been at the scene of the killing.

Justice Hodgson recommended a not guilty verdict on all counts. Hill, it emerged, had been held incommunicado for forty-eight hours and had been allowed to wear only underpants when questioned. His statements were described by Hodgson as 'fantastical', 'strange', 'make-believe' and 'a ritualistic account of the happenings'. There were no marks on Blakelock's body that could have resulted from the blows Hill was supposed to have struck.

The police were aware of this. Hodgson criticized them for failing to place Hill in the care of a local authority overnight, as is required of juveniles. Speaking of Hill, the judge made a statement that is remarkable in the light of the fate of the three men who were later convicted of Blakelock's murder: 'This case has given me sleepless nights. The treatment of the child would be oppressive enough to justify acquittal even in the case of an adult.'[46]

Mark Lambie, another juvenile, was arrested on 10 October at his house. At first he told police that he had been at home throughout the fighting. Then he admitted that he had thrown bricks at the police but argued that he had not gone near Blakelock. The state called 18-year-old Jason Cobham to testify to the contrary, but under cross-examination he agreed he had lied about this. Cobham also admitted that police had provided him with accommodation, twenty-four hour 'minding' and money – enough to pay most of his bills. At the direction of the judge the court discharged Lambie.

The cases of Pennant, Hill and Lambie provide ample evidence of a conspiracy by police to bring about convictions. They were acquitted – but the three other men charged with murder, all of whom received the same kind of handling, were not.

Engin Raghip, 20, was arrested on 24 October, held for

four days and interviewed ten times for a total of fifteen hours. Originally he said that he had gone to the Farm with friends and that he had thrown stones at the police. Later he claimed to have wielded a broom-handle near the body of PC Blakelock but to have been unable to get near enough to hit him. In court Raghip retracted his statements, which he said were made to appease his questioners. A witness confirmed that he and his friends had left the estate long before Blakelock's death. Raghip cannot read. He was interrogated without the benefit of representation. Following two days' detention, a magistrate ordered that a solicitor be present during further interviews, but Raghip went on to be interrogated four more times without representation. Despite this, Justice Hodgson allowed statements made during these interrogations to be seen by the jury.

Mark Braithwaite, 18, was arrested late in February 1986. Held for two days, he was interviewed without a solicitor on seven occasions for about thirteen hours. Initially he said that he had been at his girlfriend's house on 6 October 1985, later that he had seen Blakelock killed, later still that he had used a bar to hit another officer on the leg. In court, however, Braithwaite withdrew his statements, saying that they had been made under duress. A witness testified that he had been at a friend's home the entire night. The police provided no evidence to support Braithwaite's earlier admissions.

Winston Silcott, 26, was arrested on 12 October 1985. Interrogated five times over two days, he refused to answer questions in his first four interviews except to deny involvement and to say that he had been staying with his girlfriend. In his final interview Silcott was shown a photograph of somebody else. He reacted by telling police that they would get nobody to testify against him. He swore at the police and insisted that they had no evidence against him. It is even in doubt that this much was said, since Silcott refused to sign a document attributing these remarks to him. The sum total of the evidence brought by the police against Winston Silcott was their report that he had said that they had no evidence.

Asked by the Youth Association to sit in at Silcott's trial, an American judge, Margaret Burnham, observed:

The conviction of Silcott represents a serious miscarriage of justice. We have in mind the insubstantiability and ambiguous tenor of the statements he is alleged to have made to the police; the fact that he was not acting under a solicitor's advice when he made these statements; and that the Crown offered no evidence at all to corroborate the alleged 'confession' . . . To imprison a man for life on the gravest of offences – murder – on such evidence as the government offered here offends the fundamental sense of justice.[47]

During the forty-four-day trial not one witness identified any of the accused as having been at the scene of the killing. Instead the prosecution played up to the media with stories about mobs 'baying for blood', about Blakelock's body being reduced to a 'rag doll', about rioters who were 'pecking like vultures' at him and about people who wanted to 'parade his head on a pole'. Silcott was presented as a criminal mastermind who had led his underlings on a trail of violence. The result was three life sentences, with a stipulation that Silcott should serve thirty years.

The day after the verdict government Ministers attacked the bail laws under which Silcott had, before the uprising on the Farm, been allowed to 'roam free' after being charged for another murder. They wanted to make it easier in future for police to remand people in custody – even though many defendants had been remanded for months before being finally acquitted. More recently Metropolitan Police Commissioner Peter Imbert and Home Secretary Douglas Hurd have attacked the right of those arrested to have their choice of silence under questioning not to be reported in court. Should they have their way, the refusal to speak under duress will itself be regarded as evidence of guilt in all cases – as it was in the case of Winston Silcott.

The events at Broadwater Farm constitute a grisly catalogue of violence. From the stopping of Floyd Jarrett and his mother's death, through the invasion of the estate to the beatings, the interrogations, the sentences handed down to the defendants and the harassment of their relatives, the Broadwater Farm affair seems a mockery of justice.

Being under siege cannot, then, be regarded as a matter of isolated incidents or errant individuals. It is a plight that Britain's black community has to face minute by minute, day and night, from birth to grave. The myth created by government, that only black *criminals* have anything to fear from the authorities, is just that – a myth. But why has this disastrous situation arisen? In the next chapter we try to explain.

3 Racism: roots and development

Racial attacks and racial harassment do not occur in a vacuum but take place in a social and political context which can either be more or less favourable. In Britain the social and political climate is quite conducive to racial violence and harassment if for no other reason than that the breeding ground of such attacks and harassment – racism itself – is so fertile and undisturbed. Not only is the existence of racism routinely denied, but Britain has for long been a country where immigration policies have consistently defined the presence of black people as a problem whose entry and growth must be controlled.[1]

No, racial attacks do not occur in a vacuum. In September 1987, when a group of families in the Dewsbury area of West Yorkshire refocused national attention on the race issue by withdrawing their children from a predominantly Asian school, they did no more than express the views of millions. How, though, has mass racism come to be such a dominating reality in Britain?

To understand the cascade of racial violence around us, it is vital to look at current events in historical perspective. People born since the war often think that racism and racial violence are as natural to the world we live in as the earth or sky. But this unconscious standpoint, which eternalizes racism, only shrouds the reasons for its existence in mystery. It suggests that nothing can be done about the problem, that you can't change human nature – a cliché we've all heard.

Yet racial violence has moved from the sporadic to the relentless only since Britain's post-war economic expansion began to falter – that is, only since the early 1960s. Further, assaults on black people became prevalent only when racism emerged as a national issue on which elections could be won or lost. Britain's Empire had for decades created a climate in which black people were seen as inferior to whites,[2] but racism as a potent and seemingly universal social force came into the open less than thirty years ago with the advent of cross-party agreement that the immigration of black people into the UK had to be controlled.

It is not that immigration led to racism. That argument is still used today by apologists for immigration control: they mutter that bringing more blacks into the country will encourage backward elements in society to raise the level of racial tension. No, the connection between immigration and racism is more subtle than many commentators allow.

The basis of racism lay in the emergence of free-market systems based on the nation-state. With the rise of international competition, the nationalism bound up with this development took on a strongly anti-foreign tone. Yet the ideology of British supremacy – an establishment invention – became part of mass culture only with the rise of the Empire: it was the oppression of colonial peoples that gave nationalism its racist form. Then, for racism to move millions, labour migration had first to become systematic and the colonial situation reproduced within the British nation-state. Once this had happened the encounter with racial discrimination from entry onwards – or, more recently, from birth onwards – became a harsh, relentless and quite pivotal aspect of the life of black people in modern Britain.

There have been four major phases in the growth of British racism. In the century leading up to the end of the Second World War racism became established as an underlying current in Britain but did not loom large in most of society. From 1945 to 1962 it gathered momentum and became part of popular consciousness. In the years 1962 to 1979 racism acquired a real dynamic in society, backed by the state, political parties and labour-movement organizations. Racist killings reached a peak in 1979. In its latest phase, since that year, racism has become an accepted part of everyday life and, indeed, of national life. It has become respectable.

The prehistory of modern racism

Before the development of competitive, market-based wealth production in the nineteenth and twentieth centuries, race was not a political issue. Of course, racial prejudices existed on a wide scale: among village-based communities of pre-capitalist Europe, indeed, they were probably more diverse and more vicious than they are today.

But then things were very different. People were self-sufficient, inward-looking, and identified with their locality before all else, viewing strangers with caution, if not hatred. Where a narrow outlook prevailed superstition was the natural response to the strange and the unknown. Thus the inhabitants of one continental or regional area would acquire a reputation for dishonesty, those of another would be regarded as thrifty and skilled people would be held to possess magical powers. Over time some prejudices became fixed beliefs. When conflicts erupted stereotypes emerged to impress a pattern on the way in which disputes were conducted. The traditional rivalry between north and south is one example of a conflict between groups of people with firmly held parochial prejudices. In medieval Europe fear of the unfamiliar led to suspicion of people who spoke a different dialect or language, who worshipped in a different church or who had a different type of skin.

At first sight, such traditional prejudices appear to have a lot in common with modern racism. Both express antagonism between two groups of people; both rely on irrational, if not mythological, assumptions; both result in the use of force against the 'outsider'. However, there is a fundamental difference between old-fashioned prejudice and modern racism.

Prejudice was the reflex of isolated communities towards people of an alien disposition. It was characterized by its restricted focus and rarely went beyond the confines of a particular area. Because it was based on parochialism, prejudice was directed in an arbitrary and indiscriminate manner – all intruders were treated in roughly the same fashion. Prejudices also had little substantial long-term impact.

Once predominantly a feudal response to the unknown, prejudice today has little significance. Certainly, the generalization of prejudice into national feeling was, in the distant past, extremely rare. For most people on these islands the notion of pride in being British did not exist: in most cases strong local identities overrode nationalist sentiments. Fighting for the nation against the French, for example, had little popular appeal in Britain. Soldiers either joined up for a share of the loot or, more commonly, had to be compelled into service.

Contemporary political conditions are entirely dissimilar to those in which prejudice flourished. The precondition for modern racism was the existence of a mass national consciousness – patriotism.

The kind of state we know today was first established through the struggle against parochialism. The drive to accumulate capital brought together fragmented communities into nations. All local barriers were an obstacle to development; a national economy and a national market were essential to progress. It is for this reason that the first consistent nationalists were capitalist entrepreneurs. (Incidentally, it is not widely realized that Samuel Johnson's oft quoted remark, 'Patriotism is the last refuge of the scoundrel', was in fact a reactionary protest against the irresistible tide of capitalist nationalism.)

The nation-state created a framework both for economic growth and for technological breakthroughs based on a sophisticated division of labour. People's perspectives were widened by urbanization and the breakdown of the petty rural world-view – a development that undoubtedly contributed to social advance. It is ironic, therefore, that those who were once the strongest opponents of parochial prejudice, who came to power with the slogans of liberty, equality, fraternity and national unity emblazoned on their banners, should eventually go on to create modern racism – the politics of division, oppression and inequality.

In their earliest days the employers used the nation-state

to force landless peasants into factories. The state was their most important instrument, but as long as coercion was its most conspicuous feature, it enjoyed little popular support. Thus nationalism had yet to become a mass ideology. Most people saw the nation state as a repressive agency – one that was used against them.

In the late eighteenth and the early nineteenth century the British establishment had great difficulty in rallying the lower orders around what it defined as the national interest. Politicians and dignitaries were shocked by widespread enthusiasm for the French Revolution and by the manifest unpopularity of their war against Napoleon. A series of draconian laws was passed against dissent. Reaction at home and gunboat diplomacy abroad were the order of the day.

As decades passed, nationalism turned from being a watchword for progress into a rallying cry against domestic sedition and overseas adversaries. In the nineteenth century in particular it became increasingly anti-foreign in content.[3] Then and only then did race become an issue in society. No sooner had the youthful nation-state concluded its direct assistance to the accumulation of capital and given way to the classical free-market economics of *laissez-faire* than the progressive, anti-parochial aspect of nationalism disappeared. In its place emerged an ideology that justified every act of domination by Britain over other countries.

It is important to note that, at its inception, British racism was the property only of a patriotic elite. In the 1820s millions of town and city dwellers signed petitions demanding an end to slavery and mill workers boycotted cotton from the American South – despite the threat that this move posed to their own livelihoods. By the close of the nineteenth century, however, racism had permeated most sections of society and had begun to influence significant parts of the working class.

Race emerges with the colonies

In the final two decades of the nineteenth century Britain

moved to a consolidation of Empire. Yet as their business grew more international, British industrialists became more dependent than ever on the nation-state. This dependency, indeed, was replicated throughout the developed world. In Europe, the USA and Japan the quest for great-power influence prompted an explosion of national antipathies.

In the industrialized nations an imperial dynamic led to a qualitative breakthrough in the scale of production. In Britain, in particular, the plunder of colonies generated vast wealth and strengthened the *status quo*. For the first time a portion of the surplus at the disposal of big business could be used to pay for social reforms. As a result, what social status there was to be had was frequently tied to the success of Empire.

Higher living standards and social reforms helped to cohere a consensus of support for foreign domination. The nationalist views spread, infecting circles much wider than the narrow elite that it had reached in the past. For the first time a substantial fraction of workers began to identify with the nation-state: it seemed that their livelihoods, jobs and welfare depended on Britain's remaining top dog.

All this, however, meant the enslavement of Africa, Asia, Latin America and the Middle East. As a handful of wealthy nations came to run the world, the ideology that some human beings were racially superior to others gained a new legitimacy. In the colonies nationalism was not a matter simply of economic or territorial rivalries. The metropolitan powers asserted their right to colonize by treating indigenous populations as subhuman species.[4] *It was in the colonial context that the vocabulary and culture of racism acquired systematic form.* In the industrialized nations racism could certainly be encountered, but its consequences did not gain the immediacy that they had in colonial situations. With the exception of the United States, where slavery and the suppression of the Indians made race a key issue from the start, racism came into its own only with the mass migrations that have characterized the twentieth century.

Immigration generalizes racism

Racism emerged from the changing relations between the industrialized powers and regions we now know as the Third World.

To stay competitive, industry needs workers. Without workers production would grind to a halt. The demand for labour is not an even one, however. When production expands a free-market economy can provide relatively full employment and may even experience shortages of labour. But for most of the time a percentage of workers is jobless, and in periods of recession, millions are forced to look for work.

The existence of a large pool of unemployed tends to lead to a drop in real wages. In this the employers always have an interest. Thus when production went international, around the turn of the century, so too did the employers' use of the unemployed. Colonial subjects were from the beginning treated as a mobile reserve army of labour, a second-class section of a now international labour force. With a world-wide division of labour came packed ocean liners. Chinese were dispatched to Hawaii and Malaysia, Tamils to Sri Lanka and Malaysia, Indians to Fiji, South Africa and East Africa.

Labour migration not only buffeted the colonial world but also brought change to the metropolitan countries. Britain, France, Germany and the USA purchased the energies of immigrants cheap, taking care to give their 'guests' limited rights and an unmistakably subordinate social position. When their services were no longer required, dismissal and banishment were immediate. These trends were new.

Today the economically advanced nations survive only with the aid of vast numbers of immigrants. Each nation has devised its own means of restricting the immigrants' freedom. In West Germany Turkish *Gastarbeiter* are denied political rights and regularly sent home in large numbers. In France Moroccan and Algerian labourers are the target of hate campaigns and are treated brutally by employers, state officials and the police: in the 1980s thousands have been repatriated to Africa. Throughout northern Europe, indeed, there is a trend towards the victimization of immigrant labourers.

It was labour migration from the colonies that first gave racism a distinct resonance in Britain. Racism already existed as one side of John Bull nationalism, but it brought direct social consequences with it only once large-scale labour migration began. *Immigration recreated important aspects of the colonial situation within the advanced countries.* The use of black people as cheap labourers, together with a refusal to grant them democratic rights, came straight out of experience in the colonies. The gulf between the industrialized world and less developed regions was reflected in Britain through a series of formal and informal measures that highlighted the distinction between indigenous and foreign workers.

The first targets of nationalist outrage were immigrants from Ireland. After the famine of 1845–50 led tens of thousands of Irish to sail east for Liverpool, feeling against the new arrivals reached monstrous proportions. Despite the colour of their skin, Irish people were portrayed as a degenerate race apart. Cartoons, for example, depicted them as bestial. Hatred towards the Irish was shaped by two important factors. First, immigration brought to Britain the tensions of colonial Ireland – and the determined character of the movement for Irish independence provoked a frenzy not only in Liverpool or Glasgow but in Westminster circles as well. Second, British trade unions tended to see the Irish not as potential allies, deserving the same pay and working conditions as British workers, but as a threat – a tool that the employers found useful in depressing wages and frustrating strikes. As a result of this narrow trade-union outlook the British working class suffered considerably.[5]

After the Irish, Jews were the next group of nineteenth-century immigrants to be singled out for special treatment. Since Jewish immigration was numerically less significant and more localized than Irish, anti-semitism in Britain never reached the same pitch as anti-Irish chauvinism. But in certain areas, and most notoriously in the East End of London, anti-Jewish feeling ran high. Led by the Trades Union Congress (TUC), Britain's unions launched a campaign against cheap Jewish labour. Right-wing politicians denounced Jews for criminal behaviour and political conspiracy and warned that their diseases and unsanitary habits threatened the survival of the average Briton. Eventually anti-Jewish agitation led to the enactment of the 1905 Aliens Act, the first modern anti-immigrant law in Britain.

The most steadfast campaigner against Jewish immigrants and the strongest advocate of immigration controls was the TUC. Because the TUC's early stance has been maintained by Britain's official labour movement ever since, a number of commentators have concluded that it is the working class that is the most racist section of British society. How right are they?

Superficially there is much evidence to support them. After all, while unions have often seen immigrants as unwanted competitors, employers have often seen them more favourably – as pawns in their game. However, it is wrong to locate racism as a problem peculiar to the working class. It is employers, not workers, who benefit from racism. As we have seen, it is the establishment that originated racism and has clung tenaciously to it – much more so than the common people. Moreover, we should distinguish between the campaigns of the TUC, which by 1905 was a completely pro-Empire organization, and the more open attitudes of the mass of ordinary trade unionists and non-unionized workers.

Despite the considerable strength of nationalism in Britain between 1905 and 1939, race was not prominent in everyday British life. Racism existed behind the scenes but rarely intruded into public life. During the Second World War the situating of the racially segregated US Army on British soil led to new informal colour bars, but these were never backed by British whites. The episode reinforces our point that the indigenous white working class is neither the originator nor the chief bearer of responsibility for racism.

During the war certain restaurants, hotels and social clubs were declared out of bounds to black soldiers. This treatment, however, was fostered by U S Army commanders and British government ministers. Black G Is were generally more popular than white ones among white workers. Numerous studies have shown that British women were more interested in black U S soldiers as companions than in white soldiers – something that irked the U S authorities no end. War minister P. J. Grigg and Labour's Herbert Morrison, the Home Secretary, were also obsessed with this. In the autumn of 1942 the War Cabinet concluded that it was desirable 'that the people of this country should avoid being too friendly with coloured American troops.'[6] One recent writer has pointed out:

The British people, in general, were much more welcoming. They tended not to believe the stories spread by white G Is: that, for instance, black people had tails and barked like dogs. The segregation insisted on by the American authorities went against the grain, and was widely resented. One West Country farmer was reported as saying: 'I love the Americans but I don't like those white ones they've brought with them.' Pubs were said to display signs reading: 'For British people and coloured Americans only.'[7]

At a time of heightened social tension and strengthened patriotic sentiment, the 'man in the street' was more anti-racist than racist. Racial ill-feeling was much more the property of politicians than of the mass of the population.

Racism post-war: an emergent political consensus

As has been shown, racism predated the early 1960s, though what Britain had experienced before that period was racism on a relatively modest scale. More vital for our purposes here, it is party political unanimity on the need for immigration control that is the central, if generally unnoticed, backdrop to racial violence today.

Some of the current Conservative government's very first moves, following its re-election on 12 June 1987, were to disclose that a new immigration Act would soon make bringing a second wife to Britain illegal in order to prevent new immigrants from claiming social security and to deny them unemployment benefit or access to public housing. Thus were polygamy and scrounging explicitly associated with black people and deemed problems of national concern. Other black 'sins' had previously been outlined. In the last year of her second term Mrs Thatcher made it a legal requirement of visitors to Britain from Nigeria, Ghana, Bangladesh, Pakistan and India that they have a visa before setting off. Why? Because, without visa restrictions, hordes of blacks had apparently scurried into Britain 'on false pretences'. To a long list of intrinsic character defects afflicting black people mendacity was added. No charge was too outrageous to be laid at their door.

The race scares of the late 1980s are the culmination of a quarter-century of state clamp-downs on blacks. Before 1962 any Commonwealth citizen could settle in the UK. After that date not only settlement but entry itself was made more and more difficult. By 1971 legislation was so restrictive that only a trickle of blacks from overseas could come to live in the UK.

Since then, successive governments have turned from keeping blacks out to controlling those already here. In the 1970s, under both Conservative and Labour governments, deportations became a regular occurrence. The immigration police, dispassionately dubbed the 'Illegal Immigration Intelligence Unit', routinely demanded of black people that they produce their passports. The Intelligence Unit conducted notorious 'fishing raids' on workplaces harbouring illegals and encouraged housing offices, hospitals, unemployment benefit offices and academic institutions to refuse their services to those unable to prove their legal status as upright Britons.

In the 1980s these measures have been intensified. They have also been accompanied by a ruthless legislative and police offensive against inner-city black ghettos. It is nevertheless important to understand that long-standing all-party support for the basic principle of immigration control is what gives racism its current ferocity. Today's 'neutral' official guidelines to immigration officers indicate quite clearly that their job is to repel external threats:

The function of immigration control is broadly to ensure that people who wish to come to the United Kingdom from abroad are admitted only in such numbers and for such purposes as are consistent with the national interest. In detail the objectives of the control are to prevent the entry of people who are personally unacceptable, for example because of a criminal record, to protect the resident labour force and to keep the rate of immigration within limits at which it will not give rise to serious social problems.[8]

The ground rules by which British politicians operate have for years differed little from those applied at Dover or Heathrow. In the 1987 general election campaign all three main parties called for immigration control to be continued. Labour's manifesto wanted it 'firm but fair'; so did the Conservative manifesto. It is true that certain Labour MPs had, before the election, opposed some deportations and objected to certain legislative clauses on immigration control. But to the *principle* of control there was no objection.

In an otherwise divided Britain there was complete consensus about the need to keep black people out. Everybody agreed that to bring more blacks in would be to invite more lawlessness, unemployment and inner-city aggravation. How, though, did such an unwholesome and monolithic state of opinion come about? Here we need a little history.

'Pros' and 'antis', 1946–62

As early as 1946, when there were only 25,000 black people in Britain, Labour Home Secretary Chuter Ede told a Cabinet committee that he would be much happier if foreign immigration 'could be limited to entrants from the Western countries, whose traditions and social background were more nearly equal to our own'.[9] Two years later, when a boat-load of West Indians arrived on the *Empire Windrush*, a Labour MP told the Commons, 'I hope no encouragement is given to others to follow their example.'[10] In 1950 the Labour government concluded that 'serious difficulties would arise if this immigration of coloured people from British colonial possessions were to continue or to increase'. It duly set up a Cabinet committee to stop the rot. When the committee reported, it made the following point about blacks overseas:

The social services in the UK, particularly the right of which any destitute person can avail himself under the National Assistance Act, must inevitably act as a considerable attraction. We recognize that a very large increase in such migration in the future might produce a situation in the UK rendering legislation for its control essential.[11]

Here is a logic quite seminal in its significance. Blacks in the Third World are poor and so want to take advantage of Britain's more plentiful resources; these resources are finite; therefore legislative controls against immigration are essential.

It is this 'finite resources' logic that forms the kernel of the racist world-view. First promulgated by Labour figures, it was even taken up throughout the years in which manpower shortages made the recruitment of black immigrants to British jobs a vital necessity. In 1954, when secret discussions on this issue took place inside the Conservative Cabinet, Secretary of State for the Colonies Alan Lennox-Boyd sent a memo emphasizing that 'It is virtually certain that this government, or its successor, will be driven by events to enact legislation controlling the immigration of British subjects from overseas.'[12] To clarify that it was black people who were in the firing-line, the Cabinet actively considered formal discrimination against black people in employment. Home Secretary Sir David Maxwell-Fyfe concluded, however, that this would be impossible.[13] Instead control at the point of entry was considered more realistic. Although Conservative leaders were reluctant to make race an issue,[14] the Secretary of State for Commonwealth Relations, Lord Swinton, accepted that the basis for any future legislation could only be racist:

I appreciate the force of the contention that, if we are to legislate for restrictions on the entry of British subjects and their employment here, the legislation should be non-discriminatory in form. This will not, however, conceal the fact that the problem with which we are in fact concerned is that of coloured immigrants from colonial territories.[15]

To emphasize the racism underpinning the discussion, a paper on the recruitment of blacks to the Civil Service, written by Chancellor of the Exchequer Rab Butler, admitted the existence of informal colour bars in that sector. Butler noted that blacks only worked in the lowest grades of the service and that among a total of 46,000 applications for posts in 1952 only six blacks were successful. Butler concluded, therefore, that there was no need for a formal bar: it would involve 'difficulties' that were 'out of all proportion to any practical advantage'. Anyway, that a ban was operating would become public knowledge – or so he argued.[16]

Although not in government, Labour was in accord with the Conservatives' subtle approach. Its contribution was to make a case for racism on behalf of the white working class. In 1955 south London's Labour-controlled Lambeth Council argued that it was because of this constituency that West Indians would, in effect, just have to wait before they got decent housing: 'If we put the immigrants into council property, then it must be to the detriment of the people of Lambeth who have been waiting for houses for many years.'[17] In 1957 five London Labour MPs followed up by forcing a parliamentary debate on housing and immigration. While spokesmen for the Conservative government of the day, conscious of the employers' continued need for extra hands, called for no change to Britain's long tradition of letting Commonwealth citizens 'come and go as they please',[18] the debate that Labour initiated reinforced the view that immigrants were to blame for London's post-war housing shortage.[19]

It took only the succeeding year's anti-black riots in Notting Hill for doubts about Britain's capacity to accept more immigrants to spread further. The Conservative Party conference of 1958 swung round in favour of immigration control. In addition, Notting Hill's local Labour MP used the riots to mount a public denunciation of blacks: 'Some West Indians,' he said, 'make no effort to adapt themselves to the way of life here . . . Naturally there is resentment that West Indians can buy homes here.'[20] Racism was out in the open air, but the need for more black labour made immigration controls a non-starter. In the 1959 general election immigration did not become an issue: in Notting Hill, for example, Oswald Mosley lost his deposit. It was not until 1961 that laws banning immigrants were drawn up and not till 1962 that they came into effect.

Two factors gave rise to this policy shift. First, in the brief economic crisis of 1957 unemployment increased, and unskilled workers were no longer in scarce supply. As black unemployment shot up, the importing of foreign labour became less urgent. Second, politicians now saw an asset in the groundswell of nationalist hostility to blacks. The Conservatives recognized that tightening up on immigration was a gambit that could distract popular attention from their poor performance in government. Here Enoch Powell's transition was symptomatic. Between the 1950s and the 1960s Powell moved from quiet ministerial duties involving the recruitment of Caribbean workers to dramatic speeches predicting 'rivers of blood' if immigration were not checked.

At this juncture, however, there was still no real consensus about the urgency of halting immigration. Labour leader Hugh Gaitskell could still oppose controls out of nostalgia for Empire: the Conservatives, he argued, were 'betraying the Commonwealth'. The *Daily Express*, not renowned for its liberal attitudes, concurred. Its headline: 'Labour spoke for the Empire'.[21] Yet beneath their differences both 'pros' and 'antis' on immigration control saw black people as second-class citizens. The 'pros' wanted to keep blacks out; the 'antis' wanted them to stay but as part of a cheap labour force. The dispute over the issue of immigration disguised the unanimous verdict that black and white were not, and neither could nor should be, equal. This view was to have profound consequences over the next ten years.

The 1962 Commonwealth Immigrants Act made the state directly responsible for enforcing racial oppression. Race now took its place at the centre of national political life. The Act made Britain's race-relations atmosphere restrictive but arranged for Ministry of Labour entry vouchers to be issued to those blacks whose skills were needed. The Act for the first time gave immigration officers the right to refuse admission. Ownership of a UK passport no longer guaranteed right of entry into the UK. Citizens of the New Commonwealth (Pakistan, India, Bangladesh and the West Indies) could no longer enter Britain without a voucher. Thus, at a stroke, were more than 300 million British citizens in the Third World shut out. In degrading style the 1962 Act instigated three types of voucher: 'A' for skilled workers, 'B' for the semi-skilled and 'C' for the unskilled.

From this point on, black people inside Britain found their lives going from bad to worse.

The 1960s: Labour governments reinforce the consensus on the need for controls.

It was not until 1964 that Labour came to accept the need for immigration control. Like all immigration controls, the 1962 Commonwealth Immigrants Act endowed racism with respectability. It brought to the fore concerns about the threat posed by immigration and encouraged hard-line racists to take things further. Those who in 1962 opposed immigration control were soon isolated: for the great majority of the British population, the need for control was no longer at issue.

One of the key moments in Labour's transformation was the 1964 by-election at Smethwick, in which the sitting Labour MP, Patrick Gordon-Walker, lost to a Conservative and the catchy slogan 'If you want a nigger for a neighbour, vote Labour.' Gordon-Walker was an odd target: he was certainly not famous for upholding the rights of his black constituents. In 1954 he had joined other Labour MPs in calling for immigration controls. Once he was asked about the 1962 Act. He replied, 'This is a British country with British standards of behaviour. The British must come first.'[22] Gordon-Walker's defeat sent an electric shock through the Labour leadership. Roy Hattersley, defender of free immigration until 1964, won applause from Conservative backbenchers when he admitted his errors in 1965: 'Looking back on the original Act which limited the entry of Commonwealth citizens into this country I feel that the Labour Party of that time should have supported it . . . I make this point with no great joy because I was a passionate opponent of the Act.'[23]

Shortly after the Smethwick débâcle, Labour was returned to office. One of the opening gambits of the new government was to renew the 1962 Commonwealth Immigrants Act. Harold Wilson was unambiguous about the matter. He went so far as to suggest that Labour had never been in favour of free immigration: 'That we accept, and have always accepted. We must have an effective control, whatever we have.'[24]

By 1964 Labour was irrevocably committed to immigration controls. The diaries of Richard Crossman, a senior member of Wilson's Cabinet, confirm this point. In 1961 Crossman was proud that Labour had led the fight against the government's Immigration Bill. By 1964, however, he had changed his opinion. In that year he noted, with characteristic candour, that immigration could be 'the greatest potential vote loser' if the Labour Party were 'seen to be permitting a flood of immigrants to come in and blight the central areas of our cities.'[25] In 1965 the Labour government set about proving that it was strongly concerned about black immigration and that it would act firmly to stop it. The 1965 White Paper *Immigration from the Commonwealth* cut the number of entry vouchers issued each year from the Conservatives' 30,000 to Labour's preferred figure, 7,500, plus 1,000 for Maltese immigrants. This was done by abolishing 'C' vouchers for the unskilled. Once again Crossman's comments about the underlying motives for

Labour's actions are revealing. In the 1966 general election Labour won back some of the votes in the West Midlands that it had lost in 1964, to racist Conservative candidates. Writing in the wake of his party's success at the polls, Crossman had this to say about preventing more than 20,000 Commonwealth citizens from enjoying their rights and about preserving Conservative obstacles to the entry of millions of others:

This has been one of the most difficult and unpleasant jobs the government has had to do. We have become illiberal and lowered quotas at a time when we have an acute shortage of labour ... Nevertheless I am convinced that if we hadn't done this we would have been faced with certain electoral defeat in the West Midlands and the South East. Politically, fear of immigration is the most powerful undertow today.[26]

The only principle driving Labour on the race issue was opportunism. In 1968 it had yet another chance to show its colours. That year the Kenyan Asian 'crisis' erupted. The arrival of several thousands of British Asians from Kenya led Conservative back-benchers to mount a vitriolic anti-immigration campaign. Desperate to prevent blacks from coming into Britain, civil servants made a series of anxious but unsuccessful visits to Kenya. When it became clear that their efforts had failed, the Labour Party panicked, drew up the 1968 Commonwealth Immigrants Act and rushed it through Parliament in just three days. In a landmark decision Labour enforced a tight quota on the entry of British Asians from Kenya – because they were Asians. *The Times* commented: 'The Labour Party now has a new ideology. It does not any longer profess to believe in the equality of man. It does not even believe in the equality of British citizens. It believes in the equality of white British citizens.'[27]

The significance of the 1968 Commonwealth Immigrants Act was that it implicitly introduced the concept of *patriality*. Kenyan Asians were excluded, formally because their parents or grandparents had not been born in the UK but in practice because they were black. Citizens of the UK and Colonial Territories, as defined by the 1948 Nationality Act, became subject to immigration control unless they could show that they, or at least one parent or grandparent, had been born in the United Kingdom. Even then a voucher for entry was a necessity for most. For the first time the place of birth of immigrants, their parents and their grandparents became a legal matter. Unless 'British blood' could be proved, immigrants could not be assured of getting into the United Kingdom. The whole legal apparatus clearly favoured white Commonwealth citizens (Australians, Canadians, etc.) and just as clearly excluded black ones from the Third World.

Labour had earlier joined the Conservative-led racist consensus on immigration legislation. Now it became an architect of that consensus in its own right. By the time of the 1970 general election, race no longer divided the two major parties. It was not debated at the polls.

Anti-immigrant bipartisanship in the 1970s

The newly elected Conservative government carried on where Labour had left off. It introduced a new Immigration Act.

The 1971 Immigration Act did away with entry vouchers. Instead it formally and explicitly named as 'patrials' those persons not subject to control. Patrials were 'citizens of the UK and Colonial Territories' whose parents or grandparents, or who themselves, had been adopted, naturalized or registered in the UK. The main result of this Act was to reduce immigration to negligible proportions: only dependants of existing immigrants continued to settle. In other words, 'primary' immigration ended, leaving only the 'secondary' sort to continue.

In 1972, before the new Act came into force, the Conservative government took measures to ensure that of the 50,000 Ugandan Asians entitled to come to Britain only a much smaller number would be allowed in. Eventually 27,000 entered the country. For some people even this figure was too high. Boosted by important recruits from the

Conservative Party, Britain's ultra-reactionary National Front began a rise to prominence.

As Britain moved right in the 1970s, so the effects of Labour bipartisanship with the Conservatives on immigration became more evident. In 1976 Labour's Bob Mellish, MP, a former government chief whip, summed up the prevailing British wisdom on immigration for the *Daily Express*. His terms were vivid:

I am not a racist but I am not a humbug. This tiny island of ours is not much more than a dot on the map and the time has come to face the problem. It won't go away . . . We're bulging with more than a million unemployed, there's shortage of housing, and every family in the land, just about, is battling to maintain standards . . . My views are not really different than Labour's policy over the years. We instituted the voucher system and that, after all, is a system of entry control. I am opposed to the floodgates being opened so that everyone can come crowding in, much as I sympathize with the people who need help.[28]

In 1977 Labour, in a move that many have since forgotten, produced a Green Paper on nationality – one that formed the basis of Mrs Thatcher's duplicitous Nationality Act of four years later. Finally, in 1979, Labour Home Secretary Merlyn Rees humiliated Asians by sanctioning the compulsory medical testing, in cubicles at Heathrow Airport, of young Asian brides for 'proof' of their virginity. As early as the mid 1970s racial feeling at the rightist end of Britain's political spectrum began to dominate and lead opinion of a more liberal stripe. In particular the NF began to increase in popularity. It won more than 8 per cent of the vote at a by-election in Birmingham Stetchford in 1977 and, in the local polls of May that year, stood in ninety-one of London's ninety-two Greater London Council seats, collecting a total of 120,000 votes. Both Conservative and Labour parties began openly to express racist views in an attempt to win back the votes of those absconding to the NF camp.[29] In a famous interview conducted in 1978, when she first began campaigning for Downing Street, Margaret Thatcher said:

If we went on as we are, then by the end of the century there would be 4 million people of the New Commonwealth and Pakistan here.

Now that is an awful lot and I think it means people are really rather afraid that this country might be rather swamped by people of a different culture and, you know . . . the British character has done so much for democracy, for law, and done so much throughout the world, that if there were any fear that it might be swamped, people are going to react and be rather hostile to those coming in. So, if you want good race relations you have got to allay people's fears on numbers.[30]

The response of Labour Home Secretary Merlyn Rees was to uphold his party's record of kicking black people out of Britain. Rees reported that he had deported more than 1,100 immigrants and 'removed' a further 500 illegals. 'The exclusion figures,' he argued, 'speak for themselves.'[31]

The role of the unions

It was not only politicians who were responsible for promoting hatred of immigrants. Trade unions also played a role in this.

From the earliest days of immigration British unions have regarded foreigners as a menace to the wages and job security of their members. Racism in the unions has its roots in the desire of union officials to have a stable labour market in which to bargain. Thus when Jewish immigrants came to Britain at the turn of the century the TUC expressed its displeasure for all to hear. Then when Poles came to work in Britain's mines after the Second World War they too were made to feel unwelcome. The leader of the Communist Party of Great Britain, then an important force in the TUC, commented: 'I ask you, does it make sense that we allow 500,000 of our best young people to put their names down for emigration abroad, when at the same time we employ Poles who ought to be back in their own country . . .?'[32] Throughout the 1950s British trade unions called for immigration controls. At the transport workers' annual conference in 1957

freshly appointed General Secretary Frank Cousins summed up his organization's feelings about 'coloured immigrants': 'We cannot afford,' he said, 'that these people
should be allowed unrestricted entry into this country.'[33]

The debate about 'unrestricted entry', like that about Britain's being flooded or 'swamped' by an alien 'influx', could
not but consolidate racism in Britain. Statements such as
Cousins's could only confirm rank-and-file trade unionists
in their view that immigration was a threat. As a result,
racism became a regular feature of the everyday working
atmosphere in factories, offices and elsewhere, compounding
the deep-seated discrimination that immigrants met with at
the hands of employers. Indeed, employers, having taken
immigrants on to do jobs that indigenous workers would not,
were often pleasantly surprised to discover that unions were
frequently keener on such discrimination than they.

Even in the 1950s, when there was still a shortage of labour,
unions began to organize against the employment of black
workers in skilled and supervisory jobs. In most cases the
issue of competition for jobs acquired a racial dynamic and
quickly extended from union offices down to workplace level.
In the Midlands for example, unions agitated to preserve jobs
in services for whites only. Despite local criticism of its
stance, Coventry's transport union branch came out, in 1955,
with emphatic opposition to the recruitment of black drivers
and conductors: it went so far as to complain that the Indian
Workers' Association, which had roundly criticized its policy,
was 'adopting a dictatorial attitude and eventually no doubt
would like to rule the whole city'.[34]

The posture adopted by the Transport and General Workers' Union (T G W U) in Coventry was not an isolated one.
In foundries, in machine-tool factories and in the car industry
shop stewards' committees demanded that black workers be
confined to unskilled jobs. In 1961, for example, a shop stewards' committee at the Alfred Herbert machine-tools factory
in Coventry demanded limits to the promotion of black workers.[35] In the machine shop of an engineering firm in Keigh-

ley sixty-four workers came out on strike when two Pakistanis were taken on as machine operators.[36] At Leicester in 1974, when Asian workers at Imperial Typewriters came out on strike against management efforts to reduce their bonuses, local TGWU official George Bromley announced: 'They've got to learn to fit in with our ways, you know. We haven't got to fit in with theirs . . . in a civilized society the majority view will prevail. Some people must learn how things are done.'[37] Leicester TGWU chairman Bill Batstone was even more direct: 'Sooner or later somebody had to stand up and be counted. The Asians cannot come here and make their own rules.'[38] Not surprisingly, the strikers lost. The barely disguised racism of the TGWU made their isolation from mainstream labour-movement support complete.

In 1978 the TUC's Hotel and Catering Committee went to remarkable lengths to defend what it regarded as the interests of its members. It argued that the police, the newly named Immigration Service Intelligence Unit and other authorities should be 'afforded substantially more resources to trace overstayers' and to 'tackle all aspects of illegal immigration'. The TUC committee also agreed to tell Home Secretary Merlyn Rees that his proposal to manipulate Britain's National Insurance system so as to identify immigrants without authority to work was 'worthy of further consideration'; it agreed too to recommend that the government should provide 'more resources' to 'improve enforcement'.[39]

Right-wing elements in the leadership of Britain's unions, then, had no compunction in calling for tougher state surveillance and harassment of immigrant workers. But in practice the conduct of officials who were members of left-wing unions was little better. In 1979 a court investigating a Birmingham factory found the union of Furniture, Timber and Allied Tradesmen, one well known for the degree of Communist Party influence within it, guilty of colluding with employers to discriminate against Asian employees.[40] Two years later, in 1981, a similar court decision was made in the case of two relatively senior members of the engineering union, the

AUEW, which was still a left-wing union at that time. The court decided that managers at the British Leyland (BL) Castle Bromwich car plant had acted on racial grounds in refusing a black man a job – but it also implicated a pair of AUEW shop stewards in the managers' actions. BL's defence was that the stewards refused to work with the black man: they, not the company, had discriminated against him. The BL judgment uncovered active trade-union support for informal colour bars in British industry. One worker at Ford's Dagenham plant spells out what this means in vivid terms:

The Ford management has used racism to build its huge empire. The unions have the power to do something about it but only if we have a different leadership. I've been at Ford's for over ten years, and during that time there has been no improvement. Black workers have the worst jobs on the line and in the foundry. We are pushed around and abused by white foremen. Some years ago there were big fights. They were racial – black workers responding to abuse. The unions didn't do anything: in fact they went out of their way to deny that the fights were motivated by racial abuse.[41]

Unpalatable though it may be, the fact is that British unions have done more to spread racism than to end it. Of course, the TUC and its affiliates have grown more careful. Before now they have produced pamphlets on equal opportunities and even today occasionally claim to abhor racism. Yet there have been no campaigns against immigration controls or informal colour bars. Moreover, when unions *have* defended black workers under attack, their preference has been to highlight cases of individual plight at the expense of tackling the general racism encouraged by this country's legislation.

So long as black workers are chained to the most lowly paid, least attractive jobs in Britain, the unions' willingness to challenge discrimination must remain suspect. From the Attlee government to the BL shop steward, consensus on the undesirability of immigration and immigrants means that racism is now so entrenched in this country that it goes largely unnoticed. Racist attacks take place on an enormous scale, but apparently they rarely rear their head as an issue to be concerned about. In the 1980s three Conservative administrations have played a big part in this.

Race in the 1980s: the Conservatives up the stakes

The Nationality Act and its consequences

The use of immigration scares has been a key plank in Conservative policy. The Conservatives swept to power in 1979 on a wave of popular support for tighter immigration controls. Their election manifesto promised to 'end persistent fears about levels of immigration' and contained proposals for a tough quota system, restrictions on the rights of dependants to enter the country, a register of dependants, 'firm action against illegal immigrants' and 'help' for immigrants wishing to leave the country.[42] The significance of Conservative policy was that it aimed not to stem the minuscule numbers of immigrants coming into Britain but to create a system of internal surveillance and control over blacks already in this country. Here the implementation of another key manifesto promise – to introduce a new Nationality Act – played a vital role.

We have already noted the Labourist origins of Mrs Thatcher's 1981 Nationality Act; it only remains for us to explain why the term we applied to it – duplicitous – is accurate. Formally the Act brought Britain's nationality rules into line with its immigration laws and, in this respect, represented a helpful rationalization of the two. In practice, however, the purpose of the Act was to surround blacks with a maze of nationality definitions complex enough both for them to feel insecure about their status and for their harassers to have *carte blanche* to act against them.

The Act ended the 1948 category of Citizen of the UK and Colonial Territories and replaced it with three separate categories of citizenship: British, British 'Dependent Territories' and British 'Overseas'. Today, as a result, a black person is a

British citizen only if he or she was a citizen of the UK and Colonial Territories and had the right of abode in the UK in 1981, when the Act became law. In other words, not only are 'patrials' the sole category of person eligible to enter the UK (because of the 1968 and 1971 immigration legislation) but they are also the sole category to have the privilege of British citizenship. Moreover, birth in the UK no longer gives an individual British citizenship by itself. Only if one of a child's parents is a British citizen or 'settled' in the UK with full rights does the child automatically become British itself. Without such a background, anybody born in Britain must register as a British citizen if he or she is to be accepted as such in law.

If all of this is confusing, so are the Nationality Act's other provisions. Thus citizens of the UK and Colonial Territories who did not have the right of abode on 1 January 1983 – the date on which the Act came into effect – are today either British Dependent Territories citizens or British Overseas citizens. 'Dependent' means being connected with a dependent territory through birth, adoption, naturalization or registration of yourself, one of your parents or one of your grandparents. 'Overseas' means being a citizen of what was once the UK and Colonial Territories, not being connected to a dependent territory but nevertheless being subject to control under the 1971 Immigration Act. Neither Dependent nor Overseas citizens today have the right to enter or to live in the UK.

The Act has had extensive consequences for all black people in Britain. Many had to register as British citizens before 31 December 1987 in order to become British. Those who failed to do so lost the right to citizenship. Poor advertising of this fact meant that many entitled to citizenship have not acquired it. All black people are now subject to cross-examination about their status and are likely to have their nationality checked regularly by schools, welfare services, health services and so on.

Dividing black people into different citizenship groups

establishes the legal framework for the practical exercise of discrimination. It also means that *all* black people are popularly perceived as foreign, irrespective of birthplace. In turn this leads to the ridiculous call to 'send them back' – a call that retains its credibility in certain circles even though a growing percentage of Britain's black population is born here.

No black person in Britain can feel secure about the future now that the Nationality Act is in operation. Rights under the 1948 Nationality Act have been removed; it also appears that it will not be long before more legislation reduces still further the right of black people to live in Britain. Above all, the Nationality Act encourages poor whites to see black people as 'outsiders' who are taking resources that are not their due. It thus incites racial violence. Between Labour's Green Paper of 1977 and the 'right of abode' cut-off date of 1 January 1983 racial attacks in Britain grew considerably in numbers and ferocity. Forty-three black and Asian people lost their lives at the hands of white racists during this period. By targeting immigrants as a problem, successive administrations have effectively allowed an atmosphere to develop in which mass harassment of blacks, widespread injury and a terrifying series of violent deaths have occurred.

Media panics about immigration

Alongside the Nationality Act Conservative regimes have instigated a media outcry each time black people in any quantity have tried to set foot on British soil. Through frequent campaigns against Asians and Africans the Conservatives have boosted their party's popularity and put pressure on their parliamentary critics. In May 1985 Conservative Home Secretary Leon Brittan spoke out against the arrival, at Heathrow Airport, of Tamil refugees from Sri Lanka. He claimed that they were a threat to British workers' jobs and living standards; and even the normally sober *Financial Times* agreed. 'The last thing the country needs,' proclaimed the paper never lost for comment, 'is a flood of new immigrants.'[43] The gutter press was more succinct.'Keep those Tamils out of here!' screamed the headline in the *Sun*.[44] For the *Daily Telegraph* the Tamils not only stole British jobs but were also 'terrorists'.[45]

Eighteen months later the Conservatives saw another opportunity when passengers from Africa and the Indian subcontinent, many with young children, were forced to sleep for days on the floor of Heathrow's Terminal Three while immigration officials considered what to do with them. The reason for the chaos was that these same officials had begun to bar many more tourists from Africa and the Indian subcontinent from entering Britain than they had previously: while an average of 277 visitors a month had been excluded between April and June 1985, the figure rose to an average of 672 between January and March 1986.[46] Nevertheless, in a customarily adroit manoeuvre the Conservatives arranged for the immigrants themselves to be blamed for the turmoil at Heathrow. They announced that they would impose visas on tourists from India, Pakistan, Bangladesh, Nigeria and Ghana and set up a special investigation squad to track down those 'illegals' who, posing as tourists, had slipped through the net to live permanently in Britain.

The rules were enforced against the Asian nations first. From the date of enforcement it would become necessary for *visitors* to the UK to get a visa before travelling. The acquisition of a visa was by no means automatic and, even when agreed, could take months to get. Alarmed by the new restrictions, hundreds of families from the Indian subcontinent then tried to enter the country legally before visas became mandatory. The tabloids went wild. 'They're still flooding in,' screamed the headline in London's *Evening Standard*.[47] 'In former times,' wrote the *Daily Mail*, 'such invasions would have been repelled by armed force.'[48] For its part the *Sun* demanded that all black immigrants be excluded for all time. 'The axe,' it claimed, using a specially vivid metaphor, 'should fall without delay.'[49] Many immigrants were thrown into detention centres like those at Harmondsworth and Ashford; still more were thrown out of the country altogether.

All this occurred on the back of scares about immigration.

Removals and deportations of black people have risen dramatically under the Conservatives. In 1978, 540 'illegal immigrants' were removed and 1,234 people deported. By 1980 the figures had shot up to 910 removals and 2,472 deportations. They have remained at this level since.[50] Perhaps the most disturbing trend is that towards mass deportations. In May 1986, for example, after helping to bomb Tripoli, the Conservatives deported 357 Libyans, arguing that they were all a threat to national security.[51]

In Britain the incidence of racist attacks has been closely related to the level of government and media-inspired mass resentment against immigration. Of the sixty-four racist murders that took place between 1970 and 1986, no fewer than fifty occurred in the five years – 1976, 1978, 1979, 1980, 1981 – when immigration scares reached fever pitch.

The day after visas were imposed on visitors from Bangladesh, Pakistan and India in 1987 racist thugs attacked an Asian-owned shop in east London and spray-painted the words '3,000 more' all over the proprietor's premises. That was a slogan taken from the previous day's headlines in the gutter press.[52] The following day a gang of white youths took out their frustrations on a mosque in Tower Hamlets. Their chant? 'Pakis out,' and 'Three thousand too many.'[53]

The Conservative propaganda war against immigrants has been overwhelmingly successful. It does much to embolden white racists in the violence that they mete out to blacks. But if Conservative laws and disinformation heighten anti-immigrant feeling, so does Cabinet-approved repression.

The chase for 'illegals', benefits and 'ethnic monitoring'

Empowered by the Conservatives' new statutes, the Metropolitan Police's Illegal Immigration Intelligence Unit (I I I U) has run riot. Between 1973, the year of its foundation, and 1978 the I I I U mounted about twenty-five 'fishing raids' on suspected illegals. Within the first six months of 1980, by contrast, the unit (under its new name) made no fewer than six such raids, each involving more than twenty arrests. Then, immediately after the fateful day of 1 January 1983, it raided more than thirty homes in London alone.

As we have seen in chapter 2, the police are all too keen to turn black victims of crime into criminals themselves. In the summer of 1985 a police inquiry into the fire-bombing of Asian families in east London was turned into a trawl for illegals. Announcing that one of their arson suspects was an Asian man with doubtful immigration status, police launched a nationwide hunt to find him. At the same time they questioned more blacks than whites. No arsonist was ever apprehended – but six or more 'illegals' were discovered.[54]

Apart from police actions in their own right, the Conservatives' great achievement has been to link a wide variety of allies in their increasing efforts to purge Britain of unwanted blacks. A passport raid on British Telecom (BT) offices in the City of London in March 1986 demonstrates how closely employers and government now co-operate in these initiatives.

Two hours before BT's night cleaners arrived thirty-six police and immigration officers entered the company's building and lay in wait. When the cleaners, nearly all of whom were black, clocked on they were herded by BT security guards into a rest-room, where they were put in front of six immigration officers who had Home Office files on all of them. One by one each worker was interrogated. The questions were unimportant – the officials already had the information in front of them. They simply wanted to catch out as many people as possible.

Eventually nineteen workers were arrested and taken for intensive questioning. Within a week two made what the Home Office called 'voluntary departures' from Britain. Others were forcibly deported.[55]

How has Britain come to such a pass? The answer is that over nearly a decade such powers as BT and the police exercised have been invoked regularly enough for them to have become regarded as normal. Almost as soon as the Conservatives came to power in 1979 they issued a circular to all London's health authorities. Delicately entitled 'Gatecrashers', the document warned hospital staff about abuse of National Health Service (NHS) facilities by illegal immigrants and encouraged checks on the status of all black patients.[56]

In 1981 the government went further, announcing plans to charge all overseas visitors for NHS facilities. Health Minister Patrick Jenkin claimed that there was 'fairly widespread abuse of the NHS by foreigners', and a modified version of the scheme came into operation in 1982.[57] The purpose of the new charges, however, was not to make money for the NHS: in their first year of operation they brought in only £374,459 of an expected £5m.[58] Rather the aim was, in the government's own words, 'the effective control of the use of the National Health Service by visitors', which was of 'great importance'.[59]

After this, passport checks became common in British hospitals. In many cases too health officials passed on information about 'undesirables' to the Home Office. In November 1979, for example, a Cypriot woman attended St Bartholomew's hospital for an appointment with a consultant surgeon. A hospital clerk, suspicious of the woman's immigration status, contacted the Department of Health and Social Security (DHSS), which in turn checked up on her through the Home Office. Within minutes Home Office computers revealed that the woman had earlier appealed against deportation. In return for this information the clerk helpfully passed on to the DHSS the woman's home address and the date of her next appointment.

When they are not being forced out of Britain, blacks are routinely refused state assistance because they cannot prove their immigration status. In 1981 a school in the London borough of Newham refused to accept two Asian children until they produced their passports.[60] A Pakistani woman

doctor was refused antenatal care for the same reason.[61]
Then in 1986 the Conservatives vetoed the recourse by
dependants of immigrants to 'public funds' in the form of
supplementary benefit, housing benefit, family income sup-
plement and housing under the Housing (Homeless Persons)
Act of 1977. That veto is being furthered through the provisions of the 1987 Immigration Bill. The 1986 regulations also
impose strict guidelines on how those dependants who have
made it to Britain can live. Fiancés from the Indian subcontinent can stay for just three months, spouses for twelve.
Good behaviour is rewarded with a twelve-month extension,
bad with deportation.

Many local authorities have taken advantage of regulations
like these to deprive blacks of their rights and, in particular,
their right to housing. Back in 1978, when Slough Council
offered a homeless woman, married to a foreigner, a loan to
leave the country rather than meet its obligation to house
her, its deputy leader acknowledged, 'This is a repatriation
scheme.'[62] In 1979 Hillingdon Council refused to house a
Kenyan Asian family and sent it off in a taxi for the Foreign
Office to deal with. More recent examples abound. In 1988
both Camden and Hammersmith councils refused to house
immigrants on the grounds that if they returned to their
country of origin, they would have a suitable home awaiting
them. Hence they were categorized as intentionally homeless
and effectively liable to deportation.

In order more easily to deny blacks benefits, Conservative
administrations have insisted that officials administering
them should 'monitor' the colour of claimants, usually
through what are known as 'visual assessments'. For more
than five years rank-and-file trade unionists at unemployment benefit offices, actively supported by Workers Against
Racism, succeeded in stopping such initiatives, but in
January 1987 the government managed to get its way in a
different arena – job centres. Since that success, several attempts have been made to spread ethnic monitoring in more
job centres, to reinstate it at unemployment benefit offices and

to introduce it into offices of the D H S S that dispense supplementary benefit. Thus in October 1987 staff at 111 job centres were told to ask black people to identify themselves as black, Asian, white or 'other' when they registered for work.[63]

Such race checks summon up parallels with South Africa's apartheid. Through them the authorities can match the ethnic origin of claimants with National Insurance numbers, laying the basis for a comprehensive, computerized record of the entire unemployed black population. With this data the government will be able to redouble its discrimination against black people. How the authorities will go about this is uncertain, but all today's trends suggest that greater discrimination in entitlement to benefit is becoming a more regular feature of British race relations.

The success of the Conservative strategy on race can be seen in the way that left-wing Labour councils, such as those of Brent, Hackney and Lambeth in London, have also introduced ethnic monitoring. The councils argue that the measure is essential because it helps to identify discrimination against blacks. It seems to us, however, that contemporary evidence of the scale of discrimination is more than enough to make extra surveys by government departments and employers unnecessary. We see no tendency on the part of the government or employers to champion the fight for the rights of black people and can only draw the conclusion that they are more likely to do the opposite. Experience demonstrates the sense of this approach. Ethnic monitoring will lead to more repression and discrimination, not less. Where discrimination is uncharted it should be anti-racists who gather figures to illustrate it. In the hands of anyone else such figures have been used only to intensify racism.

Just as the deportation and imprisonment of newly arrived immigrants lead, as we have seen, to mob revenge, so the chase for 'illegals', the refusal to grant state assistance and a sinister growth in 'monitoring' all foster unofficial racism. The same is true of open discrimination against black people under Conservative rule.

Discrimination under the Conservatives

In 1984 the government funded a Policy Studies Institute
(PSI) investigation into the circumstances facing black
people in Britain. In a passage that we believe deserves to
be quoted at length the PSI concluded:

As we systematically compare the jobs, incomes, unemployment
rates, private housing, local authority housing, local environments
and other aspects of the lives of people with different ethnic origins,
a single argument emerges in respect of the way the circumstances
of black people came to be and continue to be worse than those of
white people . . . Asian and West Indian immigrants came to Britain
not as a result of a spontaneous migratory fervour, but as a result of
the availability of jobs that offered rates of pay that were higher
than those that could be obtained by the migrants in their country
of origin. There were openings for immigrants because the expanding economy of the 1950s and early 1960s created demands for
labour that could not be satisfied from within the indigenous workforce. However, these openings were located at the lower levels of
the job market, in jobs left behind by white workers who could in
this period more easily become upwardly mobile. The result was
that even highly qualified immigrants found themselves doing
manual work, while those without qualifications were given the
very worst jobs. The same mechanism operated with regard to housing and residential area. Asians and West Indians settled in those
areas that white people were leaving, and in the poor housing stock
no longer wanted by whites who could afford to move on or who
were housed by the council . . . Many of the forces that initially
prevented immigrants obtaining better jobs and housing continued
to act in this way, and were augmented by new forces that emerged
from the reaction of the white population.

The processes of direct and indirect racial discrimination in employment operate as if to recognize the legitimacy of recruitment of
black workers to some jobs but their exclusion from others . . . The
movement of the economy into recession has also had a grave impact
on the circumstances of black people because it has eaten away part
of the narrow foothold on which many immigrant workers are forced
to rest: unemployment has disproportionately affected lower-paid
manual jobs and those in the older manufacturing industries in the
conurbations. Thus although the conditions of black people in this

country are still moulded by the historical circumstances of their settlement here, the economic imperatives that established those circumstances have disappeared. But the collapse of the demand for labour has not only created higher rates of unemployment among blacks: it has also provided extra fuel for racialism and discrimination among whites. We therefore find that many Asian and West Indian people feel that these problems have worsened.[64]

The reality of the Conservative economic miracle has been to force up unemployment in such a way as to compound discrimination against black people. Indeed, such discrimination extends from jobs through housing to health care. It is worth reviewing the evidence in these sectors, the better to flesh out the wider context of racial violence today.

Employment

According to the P S I, at least one in three British employers discriminates against black applicants for jobs, while white men on average earn £18 a week more than Asians and £20 more than West Indians.[65] In 1986 a *Labour Research* investigation into employment practices in local councils showed that in only two instances – Lambeth and Hackney – did the number of black employees begin to approach the proportion in the local population. In every case blacks were employed on the lowest grades.[66] A parliamentary Select Committee report in February 1987 came to the same conclusion.[67] Another official study has shown that while 8 per cent of white graduates remain unemployed a year after graduation, the figure is twice as high for Asians.[68]

Unemployment

In 1985 a survey of Britain's labour force by the Department of Employment showed that the rate of unemployment for West Indian men was 21 per cent, more than double the rate for white workers. For Bangladeshis and Pakistanis the figure was more than 30 per cent.[69] Today it is widely acknowledged that in many inner-city areas rates of unemployment among black youth approach 100 per cent. Nor is the situation much better in government schemes designed to hide unemployment. In October 1985 a research pamphlet by West Midlands County Council accused the Manpower Services Commission of discrimination in its Youth Training Scheme (YTS) and concluded that the YTS was 'reproducing racial disadvantage in the labour market'.

Housing

In 1982 Bengalis formed more than a quarter of the population of the London borough of Tower Hamlets. They received, however, just 5 per cent of the housing on the superior estates owned by the Greater London Council (GLC) in the area.[70] Three years later nothing had changed, despite promises of action from the GLC.[71] Since the GLC's demise the council has begun to demand the deportation of Bengali home-seekers. Surveys by the Commission for Racial Equality (CRE) have revealed similar results in Hackney and Liverpool.

The PSI has shown that while three-quarters of white council tenants live in houses, less than half of Asians do; most get by in flats. Similarly, while 5 per cent of white council tenants have more than one person to a room, 20 per cent of West Indians and 43 per cent of Asians suffer at least this level of overcrowding.[72] As for private housing, a CRE survey published in October 1985 noted that blacks were twice as likely to be refused a mortgage as whites.[73]

The NHS

A CRE report published in January 1987 showed that black doctors in Britain are confined to unpopular and low-grade jobs: nearly one in three black doctors has to make more than ten applications before he or she gets a job, and many more work as locums than do whites. Almost 70 per cent of white doctors become consultants, compared with a third of black doctors.[74] Another CRE survey has revealed similar levels of discrimination against black nurses,[75] and a survey of equal opportunity policies in health authorities has reinforced its findings.[76]

If 'caring professions' such as British medicine are deeply tainted by discrimination, it cannot surprise that uncaring British whites are tainted with something even more repellent. All that is necessary to give final impetus to this trend is for the government to hawk the equation 'black = a problem' in one more area: not only at ports or airports but also on inner-city streets, which the media portray as the chief arena of crime.

The criminalization of black youth

Under the Conservatives the most dramatic attempt to associate blacks with crime came in 1982. Then the Metropolitan Police published statistics on street robberies that purported to show that 4,967 of recent assailants had been white and 10,399 black. The press seized upon these figures with glee: 'Black violence double that by white' ran one headline.[77]

In fact, the affair was a carefully orchestrated panic. 'Mugging', the term employed by the Met to describe street robberies, was not recognized as an offence in law. It became a word that was substituted for handbag snatches, street theft of all descriptions and theft with violence. The word 'mugging' established a new image of black criminality. It provided the Met with a convenient way of reinforcing popular antipathy towards a section of society that was increasingly giving it trouble – West Indian youth. It also enabled senior policemen to suggest that these youths were making it impossible to enforce the law in areas like Brixton's Railton Road, Notting Hill's All Saints Road or Hackney's Sandringham Road. The message to white racists was implicit: 'Your prejudices are justified.'

Today drugs and music festivals have joined street robbery in the official litany of 'black crime'. In July 1986 nearly 2,000 police sealed off a large area of Brixton in 'Operation Condor', a raid for drugs carried out on Railton Road's Afro-Caribbean Club. The manoeuvre was organized with military precision; the police, many of them armed, arrived in a chartered train. Roadblocks were maintained for more than five hours. Eventually eighty-six people, mainly black, were arrested.[78] Within a month similar raids were made in Handsworth in Birmingham and in Newham. In the latter case police mounted their biggest-ever operation in the borough, carrying arms and equipping a helicopter with searchlights . . . all to raid one pub frequented by blacks.[79]

The 1987 Notting Hill Carnival was also a chance for the Conservatives to pursue their strategy of criminalization. Beforehand radio stations played jingles stressing the danger of being mugged and advising that valuables should be left at home. Afterwards Peter Imbert, the Metropolitan Police Commissioner, capitalized on the brutal murder of a street vendor among the 1 million-plus carnival-goers to launch one campaign against ownership of knives and another against 'steaming' – that is, groups of black youths rampaging through a crowd and robbing people in the process.

There is no evidence to suggest that black youths are any more prone than white youths to carrying and using knives or to collectively organized pickpocketing, purse-snatching and the like. Nevertheless many white people now believe this to be the case – and not a few too anticipate the justice that Imbert would like to dispense by themselves resorting to knife attacks on blacks.

Despite all the laws banning racial discrimination and violence, the government and the police treat black people more and more as second-class citizens. Thus are individual racists encouraged to feel that they have a free hand. Without official racism, racial attacks would not and could not take place in Britain on the scale or with the severity that they do.

The bitter truth is that since the decline of the British economy of the early 1960s every significant section of British society has gone along with this tendency. There has been no anti-racist current of any social weight. Britain's entire discussion of race has taken place on the terms of those opposed to immigrants and their children. It has therefore been relatively easy for the racist view to become legitimized – and acted upon.

In this chapter we have dwelt in some detail on the political consensus about blacks as a problem. We now turn to the other side to that consensus: the need for carefully designed political mechanisms with which to contain black rage so as to ensure that the existence of racial oppression does not destabilize the British way of life.

4 The official opponents of racism

Taking place, as it does, in the middle of a recession, the treatment meted out to black people in Britain is not just devastating for them but also symptomatic of a dangerous trend towards the politics of scapegoating. The increase in racial violence demands action against it; yet at present there is no anti-racist movement capable of providing this.

The absence of such a movement is a tragic legacy of the past twenty years – years in which a series of national administrations has managed to suppress anti-racist dissent. In this chapter we examine the inability of anti-racism, *as it currently exists*, to challenge the growth of racial violence.

The story of Britain's race-relations industry

The first thing to note about anti-racism in Britain is that it began as, and continues to be, a government-created phenomenon. At the same time as they first developed a consensus on the issue of keeping black people out of the country, politicians of all parties also concurred on the need to disperse, through their kind of anti-racism, the anger that such a divisive policy was always bound to stir up.

Speaking in 1965 in a major Commons debate on race-relations legislation, Roy Hattersley summed up establishment views on the link between immigration control and the need to contain anti-racist sentiment through a process of economic, political and social integration. Without limits to immigration, he said, integration would be 'impossible': in other words, the only way black people already on this island could ever play a full part in British society would be if their compatriots from overseas stopped coming here. At the same time Hattersley was careful to point out that immigration control without integration would be inexcusable.[1] What he meant was that for the establishment to neglect the business of absorbing anti-racist feeling would be to shirk responsibilities. Immigration control fuels racism and racial violence, which in turn fuel black alienation and social instability. Without a conscious effort to integrate blacks into the system, immigration control would, on its own, lead to urban upheaval – or so Hattersley thought.

Much later, in the aftermath of Lord Chief Justice Scarman's report on the inner-city uprisings of 1981,[2] Sir George Young, Conservative minister responsible for race relations, was even more honest than Hattersley:

We've got to back the good guys, the sensible, moderate, responsible leaders of ethnic groups. If they are seen to deliver, to get financial support from central government for urban projects, then that reinforces their standing and credibility in the community. If they don't deliver, people will turn to the militants.[3]

Young went on to say that money made available by central government would not insulate inner-city areas against economic recession: 'We have never,' he stressed, 'made out that it could do so.' Rather, the purpose of state support for black organizations was much narrower than this. At the time that Young made his statement, the *Sunday Times* carried an accurate assessment of that purpose:

The creation in Britain of a small but prosperous black middle class is now one of the government's priorities. According to its reasoning, unless this happens quickly, black working-class communities in our inner cities will lose what little confidence they might have in the economic system.[4]

Ruling circles began to accept this approach as a sensible precaution, and it is one that still prevails today. After Mrs Thatcher had declared, on the night when she won her third general election, that she would pay special attention to inner-city areas long-time Conservative guru John Biffen was quite clear about what such attention meant. It did not mean simply more money, nor even a quest for more electoral support. *The object was to quell unrest*:

I accept at once that it is a natural and proper imperative to try and restore the fortunes of the Conservative Party in the greater cities. But, that said, the overwhelming reason for trying to restore a better social and economic condition in our city centres is that without such a revival those areas would become the flashpoints for acute social dissatisfaction.

I find the case for doing something in the cities to stand wholly in its own right in social and economic terms before you even start counting your Conservative votes.[5]

British politicians have long had clear aims for the machinery of race relations. They want a quiescent black population, one that is unresponsive to the needs of those who come under attack. Not only do they single out black people as a problem, therefore, but they also seek to monopolize the framework within which black dissent is articulated.

There are quite clear colonial parallels here. In the colonies British politicians often promoted black political leaders and created toothless legislative institutions that could be trusted to pacify those who opposed London's rule. This is the historic precedent that lies behind Britain's race relations industry. Of course, the industry is superficially designed to look after the interests of black people. The problem for victims of racial violence, however, is that the industry offers no defence against their attackers. Those caught up in the officially organized anti-racist milieu today all too often ignore this. They take at face value the stated goals of the race-relations industry – equal rights for blacks – and miss its real one: containment. Rather than being out and about, responding to the needs of the situation, they spend the bulk of their time in conference with minor officials and government dignitaries.

We will argue that the race-relations industry, most of which has until very recently centred on local councils, not only fails to deal with racial violence but actually compounds it. This may surprise those well-intentioned opponents of racism who continue to work within, and have hopes for, the industry, but we believe that the construction of an effective anti-racism, one really able to counter racial violence, is urgent enough to make the point an essential one. Pride must take second place to a sober assessment of what needs to be changed if black people are to live in peace.

The race-relations industry is a mysterious beast. Most people encounter it only through tabloid accounts of 'race spies' in Brent or the 'black Mafia' in Haringey. Historically, though, the industry began life as a creation of central government. It still enjoys central government funding.

Early central government devices and the arrival of Lord Scarman

In 1965 Labour's Race Relations Act established a Race Relations Board (RRB) and Community Relations Councils (CRCs) to act as watchdogs against discrimination. These state bodies had little influence over, or contact with, the mass of black people and even less credibility with them. The RRB, it is generally acknowledged, was entirely ineffectual: during its lifespan of six years only seven of the 2,987 cases of discrimination it took up ever reached the courts.[6]

Another Race Relations Act, a decade after the first, established the Commission for Racial Equality. The CRE incorporated all previous state race-relations organizations, including the CRCs, and brought under one roof civil servants, upwardly mobile black people and trade-union officials. Its first chairman was David Lane. An old Etonian, Lane had been Conservative minister in charge of immigration at the Home Office from 1973 to 1974 and adviser to the Association of Chief Police Constables from 1975 to 1976.

The CRE did little better than the old RRB. Criticism came from all quarters: grass-roots black organizations held the body in contempt, while ministers felt it to be ineffectual as a means of defusing black anger. After 1981 an official inquiry into the CRE, held in the wake of the 'riots', acknowledged that it was irrelevant to the needs of the black community – and to those of the British establishment.[7]

The 1981 events persuaded the authorities of the need for a new layer of black activists, one that would have closer links with the black community and thus greater clout with it. As a result Michael Heseltine was dispatched to Merseyside and George Young made minister for race relations. Meanwhile the government sought out blacks who could mediate between it and the most oppressed youth in the inner cities. By allocating black projects and organizations central government funds, the Conservatives hoped to give a section of the black community a stake in the economic and political *status quo* and, by so doing, calm widespread black antipathy to police harassment.

It was Lord Scarman who, in his famous report, recommended that black people should gain a stake in the community through business, and it was he who warned that 'social stability must be secured' through a 'co-ordinated approach to inner-city problems'.[8] The government accepted his recommendations, and its policy has been guided by them ever since.

Central government initiatives of the 1980s: the Urban Programme, 'Section 11' funding, Task Forces

After 1981 the Urban Programme, the main source of special Department of the Environment funding for local authorities and for voluntary and community projects, became an important means of creating a buffer to soften black resistance. The Programme has a state-led, centralized and co-ordinated approach to inner-city problems, both racial and non-racial. It brings together central and local government and voluntary and private agencies to devise a strategy for the inner cities. Each local authority receiving Urban Programme money has to produce an 'Inner Area Programme' document, which identifies needs, policies and priorities for spending. Every strategic plan, and every project funded, must receive prior approval from the Department of the Environment.

London boroughs such as Hackney, Lambeth, Haringey, Brent, Newham, Tower Hamlets, Islington, Greenwich, Wandsworth, Hammersmith and Fulham, and Kensington and Chelsea all receive Urban Programme money. Other areas around the country with large black populations, including Birmingham, Liverpool, Manchester, Bristol and Bradford, are also in the Programme.

It is by means of the Urban Programme that the Conservatives have done much to pacify leaders of the black community. In the financial year 1981/82 £7.5 million of Urban Programme money went to projects involving black people; by 1984/85 this figure had risen to £27.6 million and by 1986 to £38.8 million.[9] The *proportion* of overall Programme funds going on black projects has risen even more dramatically. In 1981/82, 20 per cent of Programme cash for voluntary organizations went to black groups. In 1986 more than half did, though black organizations receiving grants made up only 30 per cent of the total. As a result black organizations received a larger grant than did other groups. That this came about under a government that had set its face against 'swamping' should have alerted those being courted to what was really at issue.

The Urban Programme is not the only mechanism by which the Conservatives use central government resources to entice the black community. Britain's local authorities are by law required to 'make special provision ... in consequence of the presence within their areas of substantial numbers of immigrants from the Commonwealth'. In practice this means that they can obtain extra money from the Home Office through what is known as 'Section 11' funding, after the relevant section of the Local Government Act. This money is available on condition that, in each scheme funded, half of its users are black.[10] Section 11 funding has dramatically increased in recent times.[11]

Of late, Urban Programme money has been cut – from £338 million in 1985/86 to £317 million in 1986/87. Yet, along with Section 11, the Urban Programme looks set to remain an important element in the control of metropolitan trouble spots. The reason is that, in a move to control public spending more tightly in both quantitative and political terms, the Conservatives have begun to use central government, rather than local government, as the provider of cash for grant-aided schemes.

Another central government initiative has grown in importance since the second bout of inner-city disturbances in 1985. Then renewed conflict between the black community and the police showed that what the *Sunday Times* had described as the creation of a prosperous 'black middle class' had not been achieved. A Cabinet committee, chaired by Mrs Thatcher herself, examined the problem, and both the employment minister, Lord Young, and his deputy, Kenneth Clarke, were dispatched to solve it.

In February 1987 Young and Clarke duly came up with an answer by setting up Task Forces, conceived as means of promoting black small businesses, in seven inner-city areas with a high concentration of black people: Chapeltown in Leeds, St Paul's in Bristol, Handsworth in Birmingham, Notting Hill and North Peckham in London, Moss Side in Manchester and Highfields in Leicester. Eight more Task Forces were established in April 1987.

Task Force money is limited to £1 million per project. The aim is not to pour money into the inner city but rather to create an 'enterprise culture' among black people and to co-ordinate other funding programmes.[12] A second area of Task Force activity has been to provide money aimed at creating an infrastructure for black business. In Chapeltown, for example, nearly £1 million has been spent on converting a warehouse into a design centre comprising small studios, workshops and galleries. In Liverpool £2 million has gone towards creating a business park, hotel and conference centre. The final purpose of Task Forces has been the establishment of training courses for aspiring black entrepreneurs. One scheme, set up jointly with the Industrial Society and the Manpower Services Commission, is intended to provide 'business training' for 3,000 inner-city young people. A number of job-training courses are already off the ground: in Chapeltown £93,000 has gone to provide instruction for work in banks, building societies and insurance companies. In Handsworth £55,000 has equipped a workshop for training in hairdressing, beauty therapy, food preparation and retailing.

Behind these sparkling new departures lies a more sordid reality. Many of the new enterprises are simply reliant on cheap labour.[13] Many Task Force projects work closely with discredited schemes such as the Manpower Services Commission's Community Programme, which is well known for paying the lowest possible wages. Task Force has so far failed, and failed heavily. In both Notting Hill and Peckham less than £100,000 of the 1986/87 budget of £1 million were ever spent; Highfields Task Force spent less than 10 per cent of its budget; Moss Side had more than £700,000 of its allocated £850,000 left unspent. Britain's inner-city blacks are rightly sceptical of the worth of the scheme.

It might seem ironic that a Conservative administration that constantly inveighs against public spending is nevertheless prepared to throw money at black projects. But, in fact, central government largesse is only part of a wider picture. The attempt to cultivate a layer of mediators in the black community has also been pursued vigorously through local government. Indeed, for most of the period since Lord Scarman's report this has been the main strategy of containment.

Municipal anti-racism: its foundation and basic dynamics

In the early 1980s the Conservative Party, though anxious to bridge the gap between it and the black community, was badly positioned to do so. The party of outright racism was unlikely to gain support from the ghetto. The Conservatives had had little success in cultivating a black middle class and could make no headway with black militants. David Lane had no credibility with black people; Michael Heseltine's intervention in post-riot Toxteth in 1981, which consisted mainly of proposals to plant more trees – resulting in the Liverpool Garden Festival of 1986 – ensured that he was actively resented.

Fortunately for the Conservatives, nation-wide black uprisings coincided with the establishment of radical Labour councils in many inner-city areas following the local government elections of 1981. The left-wing activists who dominated the new councils were, in the main, committed on paper to a policy of fighting racism. Clearly it was these local councils that would best be able to incorporate black disgust at physical attacks in an acceptable race-relations framework. Thus, although deploring left-Labour town halls in general, Whitehall well understood that on racial matters they, and only they, were equipped to deal with the combustible material of urban Britain.

It is worth noting that the Conservatives specifically urged local authorities to find new channels of communication with the black community. In 1981 the House of Commons Home Affairs Committee on Racial Disadvantage encouraged local authorities to 'make as much direct contact as possible with minorities' and to 'rid themselves of the notion that the local CRC is, or should be, their sole spokesman'.[14] It went on to illustrate how councils could set up means of 'communication and consultation' with ethnic groups:

Some councils have joint committees with local ethnic minority representatives, others have specialized sub committees of their functional committees with ethnic minority representation. Each council will develop its own *modus vivendi*, but none can afford to neglect the interests and concerns of its ethnic minority citizens.[15]

London, where getting on for half Britain's black population was and still is concentrated, became the key arena for municipal anti-racism. So it was that the GLC led the way in creating a race-relations industry for the conflict-ridden 1980s. To a gathering crowd of admiring black activists and anti-racists the GLC represented a new beginning. It seemed an entirely different proposition from the unpopular Community Relations Councils of the past, and the notoriety that Ken Livingstone enjoyed in the gutter press confirmed this impression. The GLC promised to eradicate racial discrimination in municipal provision and to combat racial prejudice. It promoted itself as a challenge to racist attackers.

In late 1981 Herman Ousley, the GLC's first Principal Race-relations Adviser, provided a useful outline of its approach and of the general policy of municipal anti-racism. In Ousley's view progressive local authorities should:

- adopt an equal opportunity policy statement;
- implement such a policy with positive action programmes;
- establish a race relations committee of elected members (or some other equivalent);
- appoint special race/ethnic advisers;
- agree codes of practice covering personnel matters;
- run anti-racist or racism-awareness training for existing staff;
- introduce an ethnic dimension into policy-making procedures;
- conduct consultation programmes/arrangements with local black or ethnic minority groups;
- monitor equal opportunity in employment by race or ethnic group;
- review service take-up/relevance/access for black and ethnic minority consumers;
- support programmes for black self-help initiatives (usually through grant aid);
- influence public opinion on race matters through promotional, information and publicity programmes.[16]

Ousley's proposals fall broadly into two types. First, local authorities should forge fresh links with the black community. Second, councils should, by promoting equal-opportunity policies, tackle racism within their own structures, both as employers and as providers of council services.

The politics of equal opportunities will be dealt with in the second half of this chapter. Here, though, it will be seen that Ousley's first, external focus for municipal anti-racism – funding for black and anti-racist groups – not only helped to create a new race-relations industry but also *allowed local government to finance and limit many of the political issues taken up by the black community's activists.*[17] Patronage improved the GLC's anti-racist image, made radical blacks financially reliant on the state machinery and, above all, enabled the GLC to determine the agenda of the anti-racist struggle. While London's black population still suffered abuse, injury and death, its most charismatic advocates found themselves filling out applications for grants and quarrelling over which committee to sit on.

The sponsorship of black struggles by the GLC and other local councils meant a change in the pattern of black resistance. In place of direct, militant action against racist thugs and police villainy, the struggle against racism now meant setting up working parties and participating in town-hall debates. On the streets resistance subsided. The content of the struggles also changed, and not just in Greater London. A report by Bradford Council noted that its race-relations initiatives had succeeded in narrowing the horizons of black activists: 'There is now a greater appreciation amongst the ethnic minorities of both the limitations of the local authority and its powers. Expressions of demand are now more realistic and well thought out.'[18]

As the focus for black activists shifted from riots to 'realism', Conservative efforts to get local councils to do their bidding now bore fruit. It was not so much that radicals were bought off (though some undoubtedly were) but rather that their whole outlook became shaped by the new race-relations machinery. Activists grew dependent upon council grants, resources and facilities to maintain their momentum. Oak-panelled committee rooms, dingy community centres – these became a way of life.

Even one of Britain's most incisive radical blacks, Institute of Race Relations director A. Sivanandan, succumbed to municipal anti-racism. Just after the 1981 riots Sivanandan echoed the views of most black militants. In charting the course of the black struggle in Britain he wrote approvingly of organizations that had not 'compromised with government policy or fallen prey to government hand-outs . . . or looked to the Labour Party for redress'.[19] Two years and millions of pounds later Sivanandan argued, in a speech to a G L C conference, that anti-racists should not be 'purists', should not 'stand outside'. He continued: 'We can't fight the system bare-handed. We don't have the tools, brothers and sisters; we've got to get the tools from the system itself and hope that in the process five out of ten of us don't become corrupt.'[20]

Sivanandan and others recognized the dangers inherent in the G L C strategy but could pose no alternative. Meanwhile the 'tools' which the Conservatives had helped to provide them hammered their own politics into a new shape. More and more activists became accountable not to the black community and the victims of racial violence but to the councils for which they worked. Their aspirations were moulded not by what black people needed but by what local authorities could deliver. Stafford Scott, one of the leaders of the Broadwater Farm Youth Association, expressed this clearly: 'A few months ago I would have said that all politicians were rubbish. Now I understand how the political process works and the problems they have. The Labour Party has given us workers and money and supported our call for an independent inquiry. What more can they do?'[21] The snag with Labour Party workers and money, however, was that they did not come without the stifling politics of 'moderation' on race. Indeed, the shift from the unchecked militancy of 1981 to the more sober and responsible municipal anti-racism of more recent times is well captured by considering what an 'inquiry' meant then and now.

In 1981 black activists boycotted Lord Scarman's inquiry into the Brixton riots, holding it to be an exercise in containment. In 1986, by contrast, Stafford Scott could advocate an inquiry and Labour peer Lord Gifford produce an inquiry report. Bernie Grant, then left-wing leader of Haringey Council and well on the way to becoming the MP he is today, promised to act upon that report – but what did it say? Lord Scarman was unequivocal: 'Stripped of some of its rhetoric,' he argued, its proposals were 'very much the same' as those in his report of five years before.

Inquiries dissipate emotions but never convince racists. Yet since the mid-1980s the trend for militants to turn mediators has, if anything, become more pronounced. Thus have councils compromised activists. Such are the basic dynamics of municipal anti-racism. In the pages that follow we trace these dynamics in greater detail, concentrating on the experience of the Labour-controlled GLC in the years preceding its abolition (1981–6) and on that of east London.

Municipal anti-racism in London: consult, spend, bureaucratize, professionalize

In 1982 the GLC's newly established Ethnic Minorities Unit initiated a series of meetings with local black and ethnic minority groups, the better to discover the needs of their communities. With whom did the GLC consult? On average little more than forty people at each gathering. Those attending themselves acknowledged that the GLC consultation was a fraud: it left the vast majority of black people in London untouched. Nevertheless the process allowed the GLC to target radical individuals and organizations who could help it to develop more far-reaching links.

Out of consultation emerged the basis for the GLC's funding programme. Consultation was the first step away from the old CRE towards a new, more credible and legitimate race-relations structure. It led to the coming together, at an early stage, of all the key groups that would form the core of that structure. It gave the GLC its first active municipal anti-racists, drawn from all over London.

The second stage was the launch of grant funding.[22] By

providing black community activists with titles, money, offices, computers and other signs of status, anti-racism was transformed: instead of active resistance to attacks on black people it now meant co-operation with – and, indeed, employment by – the government. In contrast to the old CRE but in line with Conservative government strategy, the GLC began devoting massive resources to voluntary organizations and to black projects in particular.

In the year 1980/81 – the last year of the Conservative GLC administration – some £5 million was dispensed to voluntary organizations. Eighteen months later after Livingstone took control of it the GLC gave out £8 million; in the final year before its demise the figure climbed to no less than £77 million.[23] Also in 1983 the GLC introduced a special 'stress borough' funding programme to help councils like Tower Hamlets, Hackney and Lambeth. In 1985/86 a further £77 million was handed over through this programme.[24] Meanwhile the GLC's Industry and Employment Committee approved grants to twenty black businesses and community enterprises; the Arts and Recreation Committee funded forty-seven black arts projects; the Planning Committee aided black community groups; and the Greater London Training Board supported seventeen organizations charged with training unemployed blacks.[25]

Money just spilled out of County Hall. In 1983/84 the Ethnic Minorities Unit dispensed more than £2.3 million to 247 groups. In its final year the GLC allocated more than £6.2 million to some 300 groups.[26] Other GLC organs also joined in. The GLC's police committee funded local groups monitoring police harassment and racist attacks. The Greater London Enterprise Board spent more than £1 million on black businesses and co-ops. Both the women's and the arts and recreation committees made substantial contributions to black groups.

Most GLC grants went to traditional organizations, such as the London Union of Youth Clubs and (more oddly) the

Duke of Edinburgh Award Scheme. Equally well favoured
were black cultural, welfare and youth organizations and old
race-relations organizations such as the CRE and the CRCs,
particularly in boroughs such as Ealing, Enfield, Bexley and
Harrow, where black organizations were poorly developed.[27]
The increasing availability of grants not only meant funds
for already existing groups; it also led to the spawning of new
ones. As a result a whole layer of black activists indentured
to the GLC emerged.

To gain the support of the GLC, as of any other council, a
project or group had to show grace and to win favour. To
turn County Hall backing into hard cash involved the extensive personal lobbying of council officers, for it was only
they who could get approval for funds. The effect was to
ensure that anti-racist groups became completely dependent
on County Hall. Down at street level this dependence
weighed heavily on every group considering how to pursue
issues within its locality. Any actions that the GLC might
disapprove of were thought about extremely carefully and, in
most cases, ruled out. With the GLC the government had
unwittingly constructed the perfect trap. It did not coerce
activists overtly – rather, it was the concern of these activists
to maintain patronage that resulted in the effective containment of the black community. What was a political strategy
constructed at the highest levels of central government, as we
have seen, appeared to local activists to be merely the result
of their own pragmatic decisions – decisions based on the
need to keep cash rolling in.

The third phase of municipal anti-racism in London was
the nurturing of a bureaucracy whose sole job was to contain
the capital's response to racial violence.

Take London's Hackney as an example. In 1979 there
were fewer than a dozen black community groups in Hackney. Today there are more than 300, all reliant on council
hand-outs. The council has used an explosion of projects to
create a new black leadership answerable to its funding body.
Moreover, it has also centralized this stratum by creating

umbrella organizations for the whole of Hackney's black community.

Initially Hackney Council looked to old race-relations machinery to act as a sounding-board. The local CRE played a significant role in picking out the projects to be funded; it benefited from the council's generosity itself and today employs more than thirty staff. Hackney CRE also acted as the umbrella body for black organizations. Because Labour councillors wanted to co-opt black representatives on to their multiplying council committees, they asked Hackney CRE to organize the elections for those blacks who wanted to be drafted on to the decision-making apparatus of the local council.

Although the CRE was useful, the council eventually set up its own umbrella organizations. At first it arranged forums for different ethnic groups such as the Hackney African Organization, the Hackney Asian Association and so on. In 1983 it gathered all the blacks co-opted on to different council committees into the Hackney Ethnic Minorities Alliance (HEMA) and invested that body with the right to organize any subsequent election of co-optees. The council has thus arranged for black 'representatives', themselves first chosen through a council-funded body, to become the forum for selecting all further 'representatives'. This is quite an achievement. HEMA has allowed Hackney to draw a layer of black activists into alliance ... with itself. At the same time it has acted as a filter, ensuring that only those people acceptable to the council become co-opted on to its committees.

Alongside GLC consultation and GLC grants, then, a select bureaucracy was set in motion. Yet it was in the nature of the umbrella groups established that they were utterly removed from the black community.

The fourth movement in municipal anti-racism in London was the professionalization of the bureaucracy already formed. This meant founding council race-relations committees, as well as informal agencies, for the promotion of equal opportunities.

Over the past decade most London councils have turned their temporary race-relations working parties into permanent standing committees. Working parties brought together council officers, council members and representatives from black groups: they had little power or influence, and the black representatives on them were usually seen as 'Uncle Tom' figures. Standing committees, by contrast, have been much more successful in integrating black activists.

Blacks and other minorities get on to these committees by being co-opted. Camden's Race and Community Relations Committee has one representative co-opted from each of the following bodies: the Irish Centre, the Cypriot Centre, the Afro-Caribbean Organization, the Bengali Workers' Action Group, the Chinese Centre, the Black Women's Working Group and the Camden Committee for Community Relations. Likewise the six black people on Lewisham's Race Relations Committee come from its Council for Community Relations and five black groups in the borough. All of these groups receive funds from the council.[28]

In many cases black representatives are also co-opted on to other council committees. In Lewisham there is one black representative on all committees. In Hackney there are three – an Asian, an Afro-Caribbean and a Cypriot. Hackney has been careful to ensure, however, that blacks do not have too much power. Blacks are excluded from the all-powerful Policy and Resources Committee, which controls Hackney's financial and staffing resources. Nor are they on the Policy and Resources Committee's secret offshoots, such as its Budget, Campaign and Capital Programme sub-committees.[29]

These committees and informal agencies house-train a much wider layer of London's black community than would be possible through race-relations committees alone. They acquaint black activists with the exigencies of local politics and the limits to local funds. They scrupulously avoid the issue of racial violence.

Another mechanism for professionalizing the race-relations bureaucracy was the employment of some of its members in especially designated units or as 'race-relations advisers'. Most of London's race-relations committees have established race-relations units, complete with full-time staff, both to service them and to implement council policy. Black activists who began their careers in radical community groups funded by local authorities have tended to wind up in these posts. Hackney's Race Relations Unit, set up in 1982 with six members of staff, now occupies the most prestigious offices in the Town Hall: the best organizers from the CRE and from local black groups have been hand-picked to build a large department.

The devastating impact of municipal anti-racism is perhaps most apparent in east London, if only because, from the 1930s onwards, the area has had a tradition both of racial violence and of militant opposition to it. Back in 1976 local black groups formed the Anti-racist Committee of Asians in East London and, in Tower Hamlets, marched from Brick Lane to Leman Street police station to denounce racist attacks and police harassment. At the same time militant youth organizations, such as the Bangladeshi Youth Association and the Bangladeshi Youth Movement, emerged to provide physical defence against the racists. On 17 July 1978, 20,000 Bengalis came out on a protest strike against racist attacks and murders. Large and vocal outcries met the murder of Altab Ali in 1978, that of Akhtar Ali Baig in 1980 and those of the Khan family in 1981. In Newham local black youth agitated against racial attacks and police hooliganism and formed the Newham 7 and Newham 8 Defence campaigns. In Hackney the notorious Stoke Newington police station became the target of militant protests.

Today the situation is completely different. Municipal anti-racism has impressed upon yesterday's militant blacks that taking to the streets is old-fashioned and that career moves in local government are the main prospect for the future. In August 1985 barely 200 people attended a march in Tower Hamlets to show their anger over an unprecedented spate of racist firebombings in the area. In March 1987, after the sentencing of Winston Silcott, fewer than a hundred came to a picket of Tottenham police station, and most of them were whites employed in the race-relations industry. Fewer still bothered when Trevor Ferguson was half-blinded in a racist attack or when Trevor Monerville was half-paralysed in police custody.

The radical black journal *Race Today* has asked: 'What has happened to the political leadership which ought to come from within the ranks of young blacks?'[30] The answer is that black political leadership has disappeared from the neighbourhood and has emerged in the endless corridors of local government. It has been quangoized.

Today the great majority of anti-racist groups in east London are on the payroll of a local council. The process was begun by the G L C and, since its demise, has been continued by local councils. Organizations that were created as a result of spontaneous black anger against racists and that often gave vent too to a profound hostility toward the council, have all been recruited into the municipal framework. Equally London councils not only financed durable anti-racist *organizations*; they also backed more shortlived *campaigns*. As a consequence, even the more militant of these have effectively expired.

The record of municipal anti-racism in London shows that councils cannot protect black victims of racial violence. Although they do not carry police truncheons, councils still divide and harass black people. They discriminate against black employees and users of services just as much as the private sector does in its operations. For all the G L C's courting of black activists, therefore, ordinary black people gained nothing from it, as we shall see.

The circus-like character of municipal anti-racism is, however, not confined to London or its eastern annex. This much has become apparent in a series of disputes over the role and status of black race-relations advisers employed by local government in the provinces. Between 1985 and 1987 in-fighting over such experts in Liverpool and Bristol showed just how widespread systems of race relations are in Britain today. Despite its weight in the capital, municipal anti-racism is a dangerous *national* phenomenon.

Consensus and witchhunts

On top of Britain's longstanding consensus in favour of immigration control, a remarkable new political consensus has developed over the past five years. Today the issue of race relations is very much a part of mainstream politics. From the Conservative Bow Group's *Improving Our Inner Cities*, through the Church of England's *Faith in the City* and the Roman Catholic *With You in Spirit?*, to the Liberals' *Promoting Greater Involvement*, countless reports have put forward policies for improving race relations. All have advocated that local government implement these policies. The remarkable characteristic of every document, as of earlier ones such as the GLC's *Future Strategy Report*, is that their component parts are almost entirely interchangeable. The differences between them are only ones of emphasis and tone.

Although left-Labour councils are politically unpopular, right-wing Conservative ones agree with them on the principle of integrating the black community. The following letter to the *Guardian*, for example, is worth quoting in full. It comes from Conservative-controlled Merton Council:

The council's policy for combating racism on housing estates includes funding the employment of a project worker whose job includes addressing racial harassment problems. The authority is also committed to making its services accessible to all residents of our multi-cultural borough and tries to stamp out racial harassment and racial attacks.

New finance from the council's budget is being allocated for staff working in the community to tackle racial harassment as well as to support the interests of the ethnic minority communities. The council's grants programmes will allocate £2 million to the voluntary sector this year. Over 10 per cent of this is for schemes managed by black groups. This programme includes a Racial Harassment Unit (£22,000), the Community Relations Council (£50,000), the Pakistan Welfare Centre (£90,000) and the Victims Support Service (£21,000).

The Section 11 Programme is being expanded with new posts in housing, social services and libraries as well as an Economic Development Officer (ethnic minorities business advice), a policy co-ordinator (race relations), a translation and interpretation co-ordinator and an Asian elderly development worker, plus a number of staff from the proposed community centre for ethnic minorities and other voluntary organizations.

Merton council set up a police community consultative group in 1982 and was among the first authorities in the country to do so. This group, which contains strong representation from black and Asian people, regularly monitors racial harassment and incident statistics. It also took the initiative to set up a joint consultative committee in 1984 bringing together ethnic minority groups with leading councillors and officers. This group has been fully consulted and has expressed support for a range of new provision funded by the council including the proposed Community Centre.

These measures, and others which have been taken, are being reviewed regularly to ensure their effectiveness.[31]

In contrast to Merton, Brent Council has a reputation for being run by the 'loony left'. What is striking about Brent's policies, however, is not their lurch towards radicalism but their continuity. From 1973 to 1983 the council was run by Labour; a defection of a black Labour councillor to the Conservatives then gave the Conservatives the balance of power. In May 1987 Labour swept back to office under Merle Amory, Britain's first black woman council leader. Through all this Brent's line on racism remained the same.

With the council evenly balanced between Labour and Conservative and 60 per cent of the population black, race issues have always had a high profile in Brent. Both parties have fought hard for the black vote. As a result Brent's Conservatives have been forced to implement policies on race that local Labour figures deem 'progressive'. Most of Brent's race-relations edicts were introduced under the Conservatives – including, as it happens, one under which Maureen McGoldrick, a local headmistress with an unobjectionable record on race, was made the subject of an outrageous suspension. The initial request for 'race advisers' in the classrooms was also made by Brent's Conservatives.

The problem for the British establishment, however, is that neither Labour nor the Conservatives have come up with real solutions to black unrest over the past five years. All that has changed is the willingness of both parties to ingratiate themselves with the black community. In London, from Haringey to Merton, there is general unanimity that local councils should play a major role in developing a race-relations strategy for Britain. But as the municipal anti-racists have multiplied, become more distant from their constituents and more costly to maintain, so this unanimity has itself been dragged rightwards. As a result the race-relations industry's most recent *coup* has been to withdraw support from some of the very community groups that it once set up – and to close a number of them down.

Since the abolition of the GLC and the squeeze on finance from central government, many councils have been faced with bills for maintaining and subduing black activists that they cannot meet. Yet, since they have already succeeded in pulling the most able of these activists right into the heart of their machinery, councils now feel the time is right to dispense with the services of others.[32]

To sum up: in Britain a few thousand black and white politicians and administrators have been won round to acquiescence in the harassment of more than 2 million people. This is the logic of Roy Hattersley's immigration control, 'integration' and George Young's efforts to win black people away from the 'militants'. Altogether the story of Britain's race-relations sector is the story of a bogus alternative to practical action against racial violence. More seriously, its result has been to reinforce the grip of racism as a result of the misguided means that it has chosen of responding to it. The impact of this, moreover, has been most damaging at local rather than national level. It is therefore to the politics of municipal anti-racism that we now turn.

The politics of municipal anti-racism

Discredit to our cause

The problem presented to black people by the municipal race-relations industry is not merely the numbing of community groups or the defusing of campaigns. During most of the 1980s the gutter press has sold laughs by ridiculing the anti-racist policies of 'loony-left' councils. To underline the point that no sane person would ever associate him- or herself with the fight against racism it has seized on a series of incidents, some imaginary, some real. We set out below several real examples.

● *December 1983, Lambeth.* The Social Services Committee spends £25,000 to buy special black dolls for the borough's nurseries. This follows an incident in which the committee's chair, Janet Boateng, expresses 'concern' about black children being forced to play with white dolls. 'If they can play only with white toys,' she argues, 'they will grow up with images of a white-dominated society. They should have toys which reflect a multi-racial society.' The dolls, complete with 'authentic negroid features and hair', are specially imported from Italy at a cost of £30 each. Lambeth's Social Services Committee also authorizes the purchase of jigsaws and picture-books depicting black people and African musical instruments.[33]

● *January 1984, GLC.* The Ethnic Minorities Unit announces the production of an 'anti-racist space-fantasy video game'. Cost? £20,000. Among the game's questions: 'Do you think blacks are in the best housing?' Players answering 'yes' see their spaceships disintegrating on the screen, hear a loud computer-generated musical raspberry and realize that their journey to the stars is over.

● *January 1984, Camden.* The council's Race and Community Relations Working Party suggests that Cecil Rhodes House, the name of a block of council flats in King's Cross, is 'racist'; it resolves that the block should be renamed as a 'contribution to the Greater London Council's anti-racist campaign'.[34]

● *August 1985, Islington.* The council advertises for an 'anti-racist adviser' for children of pre-school age. According to the advertisement, applicants for the post need a grasp of racism and 'a clear idea of how strategies can be developed to challenge it in the field of under-5s'.[35]

● *September 1985, Inner London Education Authority.* The Authority's anti-racist strategy advisory group declares Rupert Bear books racist.[36] This follows several years during which attempts have been made to censor 'offensive' books including Mark Twain's *Huckleberry Finn*.

The renaming of streets and public buildings has been a consistent feature of municipal anti-racism. Camden Council created a Mandela Street in the borough 'to encourage people to live in harmony with each other and to find peaceful solutions to problems'.[37] Hackney gave Britannia Walk a new name – Shaheed-e-Azam Bhagot Singh Avenue – amid great controversy and, in honour of the West Indian writer, established the C.L.R. James Library in Dalston. Lambeth named roads after Bob Marley and Marcus Garvey. In February 1984 Camden Works Department celebrated the GLC's anti-racist year by suggesting that its dustcarts should be named after prominent black leaders such as Nelson Mandela, Malcolm X and Martin Luther King.[38]

Alongside the renaming of streets councils have made the exorcising of racist language a prominent issue. In Sheffield the Race Equality Officer, Jim Baker, prepared a list of alternatives for words like 'black market', 'blackmail', 'black list' and 'black spot' after the local council, in June 1986, ordered its employees not to use phrases that included the word 'black'. Southwark Council has produced a similar list. In

February 1986 it was reported that Hackney Council was 'discouraging' playgroups and nurseries from using the well-known rhyme 'Baa Baa Black Sheep' because it reinforced 'a derogatory and subservient use of the word black among youngsters'.[39]

The struggle against golliwogs has been particularly important to municipal anti-racism. Lewisham Council spent £15,000 on a video to combat the influence of the golliwog. The GLC banned Robertson's jam and marmalade from its canteens because the firm used the golliwog as a branding device. Hackney's Race Relations Unit pressured Liberty's, the West End store, to abandon its range of golliwog products.[40] Similarly the publishers Jonathan Cape bowed to pressure in February 1988 and created a 'non-racist' version of Hugh Lofting's *Dr Dolittle* – one in which Prince Dumpo, a black African who wants to be white, no longer appears.[41]

What attitude should genuine anti-racists have to antics like these? Of course the way in which past colonialist glories are celebrated in the names of public buildings is racist. Of course the golliwog is a caricature. But municipal anti-racism, which substitutes for a determined fight against racial murders a few bleatings against Rupert Bear, helps to reinforce the views of its opponents. It reduces racism to its superficialities while ignoring both its political content and its lethal effects. The politics of municipal anti-racism are a caricature grosser even than the golliwog. By pursuing them in a period of growing repression and reaction, their advocates discredit genuine anti-racism. Worse – and this is the most important practical point – they have created a climate in which more white workers than ever are hostile both to black people and to the anti-racist cause.

Municipal anti-racism begins from a view of the problem that is reminiscent of classical liberalism of the seventeenth century – indeed, reminiscent almost of the Enlightenment. The political focus is on individual 'ignorance', prejudice and attitudes. In the municipal conception the problem of racism is also one that reveals the need for social, and especially educational, reform – key theme of liberalism in the early twentieth century. For the municipals racial violence has dropped out of the picture. We are no longer in a world of beatings and deportations but in one of ideas, 'modes of presentation' in the media and the imagery of advertising.

Naturally, images that depict black people as second-class are symptomatic of a racist society. However, children who are presented with images that suggest that black people are equal will have them contradicted the minute they leave the classroom and emerge into the everyday world. There they will see black people in inferior jobs and as the targets of government campaigns against muggers and illegal immigrants. There they will find that real life is not at all like the fantasies that they have been offered at school. To this extent an anti-racism that concentrates on symptoms – the dolls that children grow up with or the picture-books that they read – will leave the essence of racism untouched. It will be powerless to stop the spread of racial violence.

Municipal anti-racists have failed to understand the origins, reproduction or universal impact of racial oppression. Indeed, in so far as the municipals have a theory it is entirely compatible with the government's own.

'It's all in the head': educating against prejudice

In 1981 Margaret Thatcher's government sponsored the Rampton Inquiry into the education of black people in Britain. The inquiry argued that racism was a psychological problem afflicting the individual. The genesis of racism – government-created discrimination – was not examined; instead the inquiry attacked 'well-intentioned' racism, contending that an 'apparently sympathetic person, may, as a result of his education, experiences or environment, have negative, patronizing or stereotyped views about ethnic minority groups which may affect his attitude and behaviour towards members of those groups'.[42]

By shifting discussion about racism towards a debate about

individual prejudice Rampton could cast the real problems
of racism in British education to one side. That black children
in Britain were concentrated in poorly funded schools, with
the least well-trained teaching staff, bothered him little. He
was not interested in staff shortages in such schools or in the
racial attacks suffered by black schoolchildren, or in the like-
lihood that, on leaving, those children would join their
brothers and sisters on the dole. His inquiry made no mention
of the all-encompassing nature of government-inspired anti-
black propaganda or of how it shapes the view that white
children have of black people. Instead Rampton held the
individual solely responsible for his or her prejudices. These
prejudices were treated as if they were sad anomalies: in
truth, it is the child who does *not* have such prejudices who is
very often the odd one out.

Despite the Rampton Inquiry's liberal tone and content,
Mrs Thatcher's first administration firmly welcomed it.
Indeed, Rampton proved the catalyst for a whole number
of plans to deal with individual racial prejudice. Both the
Labour Party and the Conservatives implemented the In-
quiry's recommendations.

In 1981 Conservative-controlled Berkshire Education
Committee established an Advisory Committee for Multi-
cultural Education. Its report, *Education for Equality*, is now
the standard text for what has become known as multi-
cultural education. Through an Anti-racist Strategies Team
the Inner London Education Authority (ILEA) adopted the
Berkshire document as its own 'Policy for Equality'.[43]
What does this policy consist of?

According to Berkshire and the ILEA, racism embraced
not just discriminatory practices but also 'unequal relations
and structures of power' and 'negative beliefs and attitudes'.
The ILEA wanted 'an education service from which racism,
sexism and class discrimination and prejudice have been elim-
inated'.[44] It encouraged schools to 'reassess their work in
order to take full account of the multi-racial nature of British
society' and to use 'new teaching and learning material which

more positively reflects the culture and achievements of different racial groups'.[45] Such was the background of received
wisdom on education that led Lord Scarman, in 1981, to
urge whites to understand the 'cultural backgrounds and attitudes' of ethnic minorities[46] and David Waddington, Conservative minister for immigration, to state his commitment
to 'training' in race relations.

From Conservative statesmen to Labour Councils, everybody was agreed: racism was located not in the economic and
political foundations of British society but in the untutored
heads of individual white bigots. Labour radicals in particular
felt that local reforming administrations could mount educational initiatives to good effect. Moreover, people from all
walks of life could benefit from such initiatives. The GLC
both welcomed and developed the view that racism was an
individual problem and could be dealt with at the level of
psychology. 'A realistic programme of anti-racist activity',
according to a GLC report, would 'encourage employers
and trade unions to work for race equality' and would 'seek
commitments from the main political parties, central and
local government, and other statutory agencies to adopt race
equality programmes'.[47] Thus even those responsible for enforcing racism could have their prejudices scrubbed clean.

According to the GLC's Ethnic Minorities Unit, racism
could be defined as prejudice plus power. Prejudice was 'an
unfavourable opinion or feeling formed beforehand or without knowledge, thought or reason, often unconsciously and
on the grounds of race, colour, nationality or ethnic or
national origin'. Power was the 'ability to make things happen
or to prevent things from happening'. To eliminate racism,
therefore, the GLC advocated mounting a twin challenge: to
people's behaviour, which was 'conditioned by racially
prejudiced attitudes', and to 'institutional structures', where
power was located.[48] Let us take each of these two issues in
turn.

Prejudice was, for the municipal anti-racists, born of
'attitude-conditioning moulded by biased output through the

media, schools, school textbooks, history lessons and generational influences'.[49] Prejudice meant that one of the G L C 'key objectives' had to be to refute all racist publications and media output guilty of perpetuating bias.[50] There was another point. For the G L C's Ethnic Minorities Unit much of racism was unconscious: white people unknowingly ran into the negative images of blacks that are ever-present in society and went on to internalize racist attitudes. The struggle to expunge such attitudes from the man in the street's brain became, therefore, Item One on County Hall's agenda.

Given the significance that the G L C and other municipal anti-racists accorded individual prejudice, the task was not to fight racial violence, racist immigration controls or police brutality but rather to make the liberal reformer's plea for the capture of 'hearts and minds'. White people had to 'unlearn' their prejudices. To let everybody know when people had done their unlearning a second main G L C objective was to secure 'anti-racist commitments' from 'as many of London's inhabitants as possible'.[51] The photo-opportunity, at which liberally minded actors, celebrities and G L C officials would unveil a monument or a children's art exhibition as a tribute to their own anti-racist credentials, became a tool in the G L C's campaign to educate the masses in anti-racism. At the I L E A massive resources were devoted to displaying anti-racist commitments on hoardings, school noticeboards and elsewhere.

Turning now to institutions, we may note that the G L C's third key objective was to transform bodies that, in their work, produced 'racist and discriminatory effects'.[52] However, changing such bodies was to be effected not directly but by methods complementary to the liberal idealism we have just met.

For Herman Ousley the change had to come about not so much by active measures against 'deliberate or direct discrimination' but by disputing 'policies, practices, structures, procedures, rules and regulations' that, having developed over time, were now 'embedded in the customs and practices of the institution'. Ousley's target was 'people in powerful positions (predominantly male and white)' who had 'themselves been conditioned by racism'.[53] In institutions, therefore, the focus returned to individual mental prejudice.

For the GLC, institutions were racist because they are 'controlled by racially biased personnel'. The solution was to train existing staff to 'identify racist conditioning', so that white staff could have their racism exposed and confronted before trying to implement race-equality programmes and policies.[54] In all seriousness, the ILEA printed glossy brochures telling its employees that they should deal with racism by explaining that it was 'contrary to natural law'.[55] One can imagine the profound impact this had on young racists.

In place of real protection for black people in the firing line, the municipals offer blackboards and chalk. For them the way to fight racism is to put non-racists on the payroll and to paint a less patronizing picture of blacks. *In short, the imperative is to act as if society were not racist and hope that, by so doing, people will begin to behave accordingly.* This is a view of racism that derives from the response of the White House and US mayors to the riots that swept America's black ghettos in the 1960s.[56] What the municipals have done is to take up the stirring anti-racist example set by Lyndon Johnson and his 'Great Society' programme of token reforms. That programme eventually created a layer of middle-class blacks but left the vast majority as poor as ever. Yet our anti-racists refuse to learn its lessons.

The municipals' ideas are utopian because adopting a high moral tone, living out a spotless, anti-racist life and fulminating against whites with narrower horizons will never change the social construction of racism. Their ideas, moreover, impede the cause of genuine anti-racism. Why? Because the only effect that municipal campaigns can possibly have on their 'uneducated' targets is to reinforce them in their racist views. For the municipals, attacks on blacks do not issue from every workplace, street or housing estate. They are, rather, a consequence of poor socialization, un-modern thinking and stupidity. To deter racist thugs an education in liberal values will suffice. Attend a course on racism awareness and all will be well.

We can now understand why municipal anti-racism has run rife in British schools and why local councils themselves have tried to play the teacher. One way in which this whole approach has been consolidated is through the growing popularity of multi-cultural education.

Multi-cultural education, through which children of widely varied backgrounds learn about each other, is by itself unexceptionable: the broadest possible knowledge of different cultures is obviously a goal worth striving for. However, in recent years this kind of education has been put forward as more than just a useful addition to the student's knowledge: it has been proposed as an answer to the problem of racism. That it certainly is not.[57]

What has been applied in the classroom has been attempted in wider society – particularly by poster. In 1982 the GLC established London as an 'Anti-racist Zone' and declared 1984 an 'Anti-racist Year'. The centrepiece of its strategy was a declaratory poster campaign. 'Where would Mrs Thatcher have got to if she had been black?' asked one of the original posters. 'To the front of the housing queue,' answered racist graffiti artists, unconvinced. To confront the mental agony caused by racism another GLC campaign asked racists: 'Haven't you got enough problems already?' Lambeth Council duly plastered its walls with the sermonizing 'You would be much nicer if you weren't.'

Alongside their street-hoarding pleas local authorities set up 'racism-awareness courses' for their staff. In Newham these featured a 'variety of approaches, including experiential techniques and games'. Lewisham Racism Awareness Training Unit organized special courses for blacks so as to 'enhance and strengthen ... practices that lead to power acquisition particularly within the confines of white organizations and society in general'.[58] Meanwhile the GLC campaigned to teach white people about black culture, sponsoring black music, art, theatre and dance. In schools pupils learnt about the Koran, drew maps of India and read about Marcus Garvey. Children could now play in steel bands and not just in traditional orchestras. Racist school books were censored, and new texts were written that depicted blacks in a positive fashion.

It would be nice if eradicating racism could ever be that easy. The difficulty is that racism cannot be trained or educated away. Racist ideas are not the product of bad teachers or myopic school materials. They come about as a result of the real social conditions under which black people are forced to live. Instructing whites in black culture will not rid them of the fear that the presence of blacks in Britain makes getting a job or a house a more difficult business. It is the organized, overt racism of the authorities, not the personal upbringing of philistine individuals, that has legitimized racist ideas and racist behaviour.

The educational dynamic of the politics of municipal anti-racism has not just *diverted* people from tackling racial violence: it has actively *deterred* them from doing so. While councils have battled against 'unconscious racism', all-too-conscious racists have waged a real war on black people. In 1986 a quarter of Newham's Asian population suffered racist attacks, yet the council responded by creating a special 'hit squad' to remove racist graffiti and by sending its housing staff on yet more anti-racist training courses.

The dogma of racial 'awareness' is not just silly; it also allows local authorities to hide the truth. For all the self-satisfied liberal aura that surrounds municipal initiatives in anti-racist education, the practical function of such initiatives is to cover up the racist practices of local authorities and to serve as a pretext for attacking those who beg to take issue with it.

In education municipal anti-racism, through its pettiness and absurdity, speeds the growth of reaction. As a dramatic outburst of hostility to Asian schoolchildren in Dewsbury, West Yorkshire, has shown, multi-cultural educators and white racists tend to feed off each other.[59] The multi-cultural approach allows right-wing forces to portray all anti-racists, including those independent of the municipal circus, as 'loonies'. If, in the public's perception, being against racism is to drink 'coffee without milk' rather than 'black coffee', what sane person would call him- or herself an anti-racist, still less do something about racial violence?

The segregation of schools implicit in the Bill proposed by education minister Kenneth Baker in November 1987 promises to make the classroom just as much an arena for racial violence as the street and the council estate. But extra teaching modules on the development of slavery will not be enough to bar racial violence from playgrounds or infuriated white parents from school gates. For that to happen, the ivory-tower world of liberal educationalists will have to give way to a cold and accurate appraisal of the full extent and horror of the racial scourge.

The failure of equal opportunities in employment

Municipal anti-racists hailed Hackney and Lambeth councils as beacons of progress. In both, it is true, the proportion of blacks in the workforce has increased fourfold in the past five years. But the benefits for black people have been largely illusory. The increase in the proportion of blacks in the workforce in the two years after Hackney introduced its target system was the same as in the two years before.[60] More important, equal opportunities offered jobs only for a few hundred blacks in the borough; a quick walk down Sandringham Road, Hackney's 'front line', shows that, for the vast majority of young blacks the dole is still the only answer.

A May 1986 survey by *Labour Research* helps to put equal opportunities in perspective.[61] Apart from Hackney and Lambeth, there is not a single council workforce in which the proportion of blacks even begins to approach the local ethnic mix. Even at the GLC blacks occupied just 10 per cent of the workforce – while they made up 20 per cent of the Greater

London population. In some councils blacks face an astonishing degree of discrimination. Labour-controlled Newham, a borough in which 30 per cent of the population is black, employs fewer than 300 among a workforce of 11,000. Liverpool Council employs fewer than 300 blacks out of 30,000 council workers.

In every council surveyed by *Labour Research*, including Lambeth and Hackney, black workers were concentrated in the lowest grades. Even the 'successes' claimed by some councils were a sham. When the GLC introduced a special recruitment policy to increase the number of blacks in the fire service, the proportion increased by more than a third, but that meant a rise from 1.2 to 1.6 per cent of the total workforce. There were fewer black firemen in London at the time of the abolition of the GLC than there were under the old London County Council in 1948.

Equal opportunities in employment have worked – but only in the sense that they have divided exploited whites from oppressed blacks. For, in the midst of council cutbacks, frozen posts and declining workforces, talk of positive discrimination in favour of black people has been interpreted in the only possible way by predominantly white workforces: namely, that their members must make sacrifices so as to 'even up' the racial balance on behalf of their employers. As a result, black and white workers are set against each other.

While equal opportunities make whites resentful, many black people themselves view its corollary, 'positive discrimination', with distaste. They prefer instead to be recruited on merit, not skin colour. Conversely, whites often feel themselves the victims of those blacks who are promoted over their heads in what are often transparently obvious cases of council window-dressing. Positive discrimination produces effects that are wholly negative.

The arguments in favour of racial equality in employment are obvious. All the facts suggest, however, that it is much more likely to be achieved by a thriving, eloquent and forceful anti-racist movement, rooted in workplaces, than by Britain's local authorities. We have seen that central government promotes racism at every point, and we know that local government is now under the thumb of Whitehall after more than half a century of gentle but increasing subordination. Genuine 'equal opportunities' in hiring, promotion and recruitment, then, cannot be a gift in the hands of local government, cannot be assured by a mandatory piece of small print at the bottom of job advertisements on the public appointments pages of the *Guardian*. Equal opportunities, like freedom from racial violence, can only be *won*. This is a message that is foreign to the complacent world of municipal anti-racism but is already understood by anybody who has bothered to look at how hiring and firing really work in Britain today.

The failures over housing and racist attacks

'Equality' in municipal employment has had its counterpart in municipal housing. In 1982 a report on housing in Tower Hamlets showed that on ten estates to which Bengalis would have liked to move the proportion of black tenants was less than 5 per cent. On some estates the proportion of blacks was as low as 0.3 per cent. The report concluded: 'Effectively the GLC has picked out certain old estates on which it will make offers to Bengalis, and is keeping others almost exclusively white.'[62] Municipal anti-racists have spent much of the 1980s trying to counteract circumstances like these – but to no avail.

The Tower Hamlets report, which was written by a local housing group, accepted the GLC's contention that it could not provide decent homes for all. Instead of this the report argued for a fairer distribution of existing resources. With cuts in the budget for new housing programmes, it pointed out, the salient feature of anti-racist house-allocation policy would be that it could make at least a start, in that it could distribute fairly such housing as was available. 'This,' the report added, 'does not cost money; it only asks for a firm and continuing commitment from GLC members.'[63]

After five years of torment Nasreen still has to fight against
harassment (Pandora Anderson).

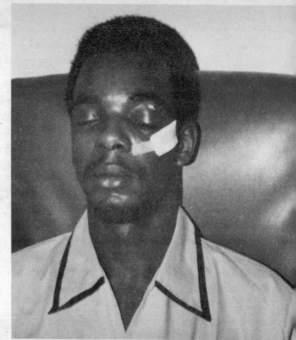

Trevor Ferguson after the removal of his left eye. His attackers are still at liberty.

Brain-damaged Trevor Monerville two days after spending time with Stoke Newington police (Pandora Anderson).

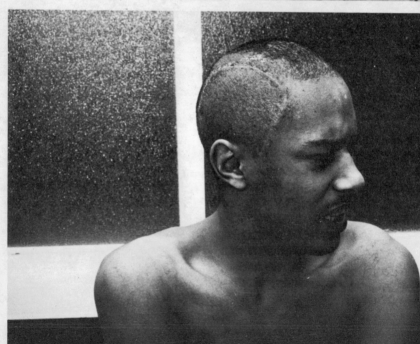

Metso Moncrieffe and Janet, his wife, on the march in Birmingham
(Dave Rourke).

George Roucou and his wife Kim lead a huge workers' demonstration through Manchester.

yd Jarrett consoles Winston Silcott's father, Walter, after the life sentence
sed on Winston. Floyd said, 'It is as if they have killed my mother all
r again' (John Voos).

Broadwater Farm residents march against the convictions meted out to Engin
Raghip, Winston Silcott and Mark Braithwaite (Pandora Anderson).

Mr Ali from Tower Hamlets, who is now living in peace thanks to a timely intervention from WAR activists.

...centration-camp-style surroundings for those refused the right
...ay in Britain (Joe Boatman).

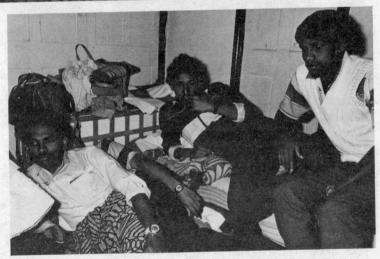

Tamils incarcerated on a prison ship at Harwich pending their
removal from the country.

Lambeth Council's attempt to fight racism.

Mayhem outside Wolverhampton's Next shop after the death of
Clinton McCurbin (Krysia Rozanska).

The GLC gave that commitment. It acted on the report, started monitoring which of its houses went to whom and set up a Race and Housing Action Team to shake things up. Two years later a fresh report observed that the situation on the estates had not changed fundamentally.[64] Just 5 per cent of allocations on Tower Hamlets' better estates went to blacks. On three brand-new estates, built in the intervening period, black allocations amounted to a princely 1 per cent. 'Somewhere, somehow,' concluded the new report, 'deliberate decisions must have been taken over which estates [Bengalis] were going to be "allowed" to live on ... Nothing said or done by the GLC administration over the last three years has changed this.'[65]

The situation is little different under other radical councils. Throughout this chapter we have stressed that municipal solutions are not 'better than nothing' but, rather, *counter-productive*. This is as true of housing as it is of education and employment. Here the example of Newham is a telling one.

In 1984 Newham Council hit the headlines when it evicted Rosina McDonnel and her three children from their council flat in Canning Town. They had been racially harassing a black neighbour. The eviction was part of Newham's new anti-racist policy, which, among other measures, involved the distribution of leaflets to every household in the borough threatening the eviction of racist tenants.

Through these actions Newham inflamed racist passions while breaking records for hypocrisy. For decades the Labour council had treated blacks in the borough as pariahs. Its housing policies had led to no-go areas and ghettos alike. More than 70 per cent of Newham Council's housing still lies in the most racist areas in the south of the borough. Because most council tenancies arise only in this area, black families who want to avoid racial harassment have little choice but to move into the private sector. In a borough where 30 per cent of the population is black, blacks are allocated just 14 per cent of council tenancies.

Until 1985 Newham operated a five-year residential qualifi-
cation for council housing, the effect of which was to lower
black people's chances of finding council accommodation.
Moreover, 85 per cent of ordinary housing transfers in 1985
went to whites. In fact, there was only one housing-allocation
category in which blacks did relatively well – transfer because
of racist harassment. Even here, however, almost 10 per cent
of allocations went to tenants who were white.[66]

Despite the best of intentions on the part of Newham Council their effect seems to be that thousands of whites in
Newham see large areas of the borough as their own. The
failure to build new houses and the subsequent squeeze on
existing stock have encouraged white tenants to hang on to
what they have more fiercely than ever before. Blacks are
seen as competitors who must be excluded. Forced out of an
all-white housing estate in south Newham, a black family was
told: 'We've never had blacks in this area and we're not
going to have any now.'[67] A council survey published in
March 1987 showed that one in four blacks in the borough
had suffered from racist attacks in the past year.

While Newham institutionalized racism through its housing policies, its eviction of the McDonnels created a racist
backlash among white tenants. Demonstrations of support
for the racist family broke out on the McDonnels' estate. Yet,
although eviction remains the policy of Newham Council, the
McDonnels have been the only racists to suffer from it. As
we have mentioned, far more common has been the lengthy
process of 'transfer' for black tenants who fall prey to racial
harassment from their neighbours. Like the McDonnels
affair, this policy too has exacerbated racial tensions.

Transferring blacks out of racist territory means that such
territory will be even more intolerable for those black families
who remain or for those who venture into it. As one housing
officer in Newham has commented, while the council may
wish to eliminate no-go areas, 'Practically, this is not
possible.'[68] Moreover, because of the enormous numbers of
black council tenants facing racist attacks, the average waiting

time for a transfer is more than six months. In those parts of Newham where the problem is particularly acute, such as Custom House, Canning Town and north Plaistow, more than a year must be endured by black tenants before the council acts.[69]

Having accepted that it has no solution to the problem of racist attacks, the council has developed a new policy – keeping blacks out of hostile areas. Thus Newham's housing department can stop black tenants from moving into white fortresses and can veto a transfer when it feels that such a move is likely to lead to racist attacks. In a manner all too reminiscent of South Africa, the council effectively dictates to black people where they can and cannot live.

To avoid the charge of ghettoizing immigrants, Newham does target some predominantly white areas into which to move its black tenants. In these locations it allows vacant council premises to remain empty until a cluster of a dozen or so dwellings builds up, then it moves black families in *en masse* to afford them protection.[70] The bleak results are clear in the statistics for racial harassment in the borough, which reveal that white tenants, reacting against Newham's sordid public-relations gestures, regularly take out their frustrations on black tenants.

The divisive consequences of municipal housing policies are not restricted to Newham. In October 1987 a CRE document, *Living in Terror*, put forward a national policy to combat the high incidence of racism on Britain's council estates. It wanted racial harassment to be recognized as worthy grounds for eviction, the 'high-priority transfer for victims where necessary' and 'regular liaison with the police on housing'.[71] But the CRE has learned nothing. It recognizes that the transfer of harassed black tenants amounts to little more than a walkover for white racists, yet it argues that the victims' individual 'choice' of where to live should be paramount. But when an iron bar is put to your door or stones are thrown through your window, you have no choice. If the alternatives are to remain under attack or to move, only a fool would remain. Given a means to stop attacks and isolate those guilty of them, many families would choose to avoid being uprooted. But municipal anti-racists, whether on the CRE or on Britain's councils, have no policy to arrange for this. As a result the transfers go on, and more racial polarization is stored up for future years.

Municipal anti-racism in today's climate of cuts

In municipal hands equality means the more even reallocation of dwindling resources. What, in turn, does this mean? A Hackney Labour councillor, John Bloom, has given an honest answer: 'We're trying,' he said in 1984, 'to find a way of ensuring that the misery is shared out equally and fairly.'[72]

In municipal politics one part of the population is forced to make sacrifices for another. Inevitably this leads white workers to regard black people as the source of their problems. It is municipal policies of 'equality' as much as a speech by Mrs Thatcher or an editorial in the *Sun* that reinforce the popular suspicion that blacks take white jobs. Instead of uniting black people and white through an independent fight *against* harassment and discrimination and *for* decent employment and housing for all, council policies heighten racial divisions.

While councils have used anti-racist rhetoric, they have also cut their expenditures. In 1985 the collapse of the campaign against rate-capping showed that Labour councils had given up doing anything about 'Tory cuts'. Several leading anti-racist councils, such as Brent, were not even threatened with rate-capping: they had done their cutting earlier. Today, however, things are even worse. Under Labour, municipal austerity has put paid to every plan for combating racism by official means. Thus although Hackney Council has created about 500 jobs for blacks, it has frozen 1,400 town-hall posts altogether.[73]

Being but the local sector of the British state, municipal authorities are as thoroughly permeated by racial discrimination as any other government body. It is ridiculous to expect agencies that enforce racism to lead the fight against it. Indeed, the recessionary late 1980s have made it clear that even arm-waving about anti-racism has had its day. In 1986 left-wing Islington Council refused to house a Turkish family, the Ozberbers, because its members had made themselves 'intentionally homeless' . . . by leaving Turkey. According to local officials, it was 'unreasonable' for the Ozberbers to 'move into an area that is already under severe housing and employment stress'.[74] A municipal aberration? Not at all. In Tower Hamlets an Alliance-dominated council has used the same argument to threaten 100 Bengalis with deportation. In Camden the same policy has been adopted. There a left-wing Labour leadership has embarked on repatriation: Irish and Bangladeshi families have been offered air tickets as an alternative to homes. As in the case of Tower Hamlets, Camden has accused such families of making themselves 'intentionally homeless'.[75]

In Camden's expulsions municipal anti-racism has met the end of the road. Labour's consensus with the Conservatives on immigration control, on the need for containment of the black community through local authority action, on the phenomenon of 'prejudice' and the need for education against it, has led to vicious 'economies' in council-provided accommodation and general services. But the story does not end there. Precisely because black council employees are also at the sharp end of the 'caring cuts', left-wing municipals have the nerve to claim that they will protect 'equal opportunities' by making more whites redundant than blacks. They then turn around and throw the charge of racism at white opponents of such cuts.

The Maureen McGoldrick affair in Brent is a disturbing example of this trend. In October 1986 Brent teachers went on strike against the suspension of McGoldrick, head of Sudbury Infants' School, for allegedly making racist remarks. A governors' inquiry had earlier cleared her, but Brent Council ruled that she had to face another disciplinary hearing, this time conducted by its members. Among council employees the black workers' group, along with many on the left, opposed the teachers' strike, supporting the council's right to 'implement its anti-racist policies'. Finally, in a remarkable and bitter about-turn, Brent backed down after education minister Kenneth Baker appeared on the scene to rescue McGoldrick, a genuine anti-racist, from its clutches.

Brent's decision to discipline McGoldrick sparked off a hysterical media campaign against the council's 'loony-left' policies. The campaign was fuelled by the subsequent news that Brent was to employ in its schools 180 'race advisers', whose job would be to tackle racism in the curriculum. Despite the fact that it was the previous Conservative administration that had proposed them, Arthur Steele, former Conservative education chief in Brent, called the race advisers 'spies in the classroom' and went on to draw parallels with the Nazis. Even BBC's *Panorama*, normally a sober programme, alleged that Brent was trying to 'censor teachers' thoughts'.

The real story behind the McGoldrick dispute reveals how cynically Britain's municipals have begun to use anti-racist rhetoric to divert attention from cuts in council spending. For Brent Council McGoldrick's real crime was not racism – there was no evidence of this – but vociferous opposition to teacher shortages and overcrowded classrooms in Brent.[76] The schools worst hit by Brent's education crisis – Sudbury, Chalkhill, Uxendon Manor, Preston Park, Oliver Goldsmith, Brentfield and Oakington Manor – were predominantly black. At Sudbury four teaching posts out of twenty-two were unfilled. Yet when McGoldrick made a written application to recruit more staff Brent Council's Education Department denied knowledge of it, claiming that it had been 'lost'. Just a week before McGoldrick was suspended, an angry meeting at her school denounced Labour councillors for failing to reverse the cuts. When Brent Council then replied by accusing McGoldrick of racism, pandemonium broke out.

Brought against a teacher who herself had long supported Brent's anti-racist policies, the charge of racism was always implausible, and the backing that McGoldrick received from black children at her school and their parents made it even less likely. Nevertheless, silencing McGoldrick offered the Labour council the means of eliminating one of the fiercest critics of its austerity policies – and, at a pinch, the chance to polish up its radical image among the black community. Brent took that chance. The council's attack on McGoldrick provoked local whites, however, making the position of blacks in the borough even more insecure. The *dénouement* of the affair was sickening too: in exonerating McGoldrick, Kenneth Baker appeared more fair-minded than the most militant municipal anti-racist. What the McGoldrick episode shows incontrovertibly is that the municipal methods can lead to disaster.

The myth of a multi-racial Britain

Behind municipal anti-racism is the belief that social engineering can create a harmonious multi-racial Britain. For years educationalists, churchmen and the TUC have urged Conservative ministers to accept that ours is, and should be officially recognized as, a multi-racial society. Although Conservatives have repeatedly demurred at this, our liberal friends greet their response with incomprehension. Why can the authorities not make more frequent denunciations of the injustice of racism and the horror of racial violence? It would be fine if racial harmony could coexist with a free-market economy – if customs officials, policemen, landlords, employers and headmasters all rushed to counter racial violence and discrimination. Unhappily, however, they do not. Such behaviour on their part would contradict the essential character of the society in which we live.

Resources are shrinking as the profits from industry shrink. In the wake of the financial crash of October 1987 the government has shown itself more willing than ever to scapegoat foreigners, arguing that the Americans, West Germans and Japanese are to blame for Britain's economic troubles. Ever since the Falklands war nearly every political issue in Britain has revolved around varying but fundamentally united party-political conceptions of national security and identity, around the threat to the country posed by Irish republicans, Libyan bombers and Soviet agents – not to speak of football fans and the sexually promiscuous. Here is how the *Financial Times* summed up its report of Mrs Thatcher's triumphant post-election address to the October 1987 Conservative Party conference:

Underlining the importance of introducing Trident submarines to modernize the deterrent, Mrs Thatcher contended that peace was only maintained by resisting violence and intimidation at home and standing up to terrorists abroad.

She said: 'That is the true spirit of the British people. It sustained them through two world wars. It guides us still.'

What price a multi-racial society in this climate? What price such a society when every British government since the 1960s has in practice shown its total commitment to 'our kith and kin' in South Africa?

Britain has played a historic role in colonizing the Third World and oppressing black people. When it left its colonies Britain installed a loyal and trusted band of black politicians and administrators. Today it makes a similar effort back home. Yet while all economic and political trends today run counter to mixing 'multi-racialism' alongside the much more fêted 'enterprise culture', those caught up in the municipal apparatus have yet to realize this fact. They have – or at least had – their little niche, and that, it seems, is all that matters to them.

Black people will be used as cheap labour in times of labour shortage and will be depicted as parasites in times of unemployment. There is no chance that any of us will ever see a truly multi-racial society unless it is one with expanding production and employment. In other words, although the fight against racial violence must begin now, it will advance most quickly as part of the fight for a completely new kind of Britain.

Every aspect of racism will have to be countered if the whole phenomenon is to be ended. The central obstacle will be government itself as the main enforcer of racial oppression. That is why genuine anti-racism is such a potentially revolutionary force. For black people really to be equal demands a transformation in the society in which we live. This also explains why governments of every stamp have been so keen to contain anti-racism. If black people and white anti-racists by the million withdrew their consent from the British state, we can be sure that one of the most severe political crises in the history of modern Britain would break out.

For black people the immediate future looks gloomier than ever. Municipal anti-racism will be powerless to help them. A new anti-racist movement, with politics that are far removed from the legacy of Lord Scarman and the mirage of a multi-racial country, is an urgent necessity. In our final chapter we look at how such a movement could be built.

5   A new anti-racist movement

Personal experience has taught me that building a new anti-racist movement will not be simple. Three Conservative governments have entrenched racism more firmly in Britain than ever before. As we have seen, the Conservatives have launched a series of propaganda offensives targeting immigrants as the cause of a multitude of British problems: declining moral standards, inner-city decay, the 'culture' of 'dependence' on state benefits and even the creation of 'impossible' working conditions for passport officers at Heathrow.

British politics has taken on a new pattern. Many people accept state clamp-downs on everyday life as legitimate and necessary. The Public Order Act limits the right to demonstrate; the Police and Criminal Evidence Act limits the rights of those in police custody. Trade-union rights have virtually disappeared, and the denial of the right to strike in the public sector is mooted more and more frequently. While Parliament decides to restrict women's right to have abortions, about the activities of the services it decides nothing. Authors, journalists, publishers, broadcasters, civil servants – each have had experience of pressure being brought to bear by Whitehall.

Any movement to oppose the state's legalized interference in the lives of black people has to contend with this general environment. It is easy to be pessimistic. However, once it is realized that Mrs Thatcher has not yet had to face a serious opposition, the prospectus changes. After all, Labour has conceded Mrs Thatcher political ground on every issue – and especially on race.

Labour has failed to oppose the drift towards a more authoritarian state because it agrees with the Conservatives on all the basic issues. When two people died in fighting between police and black youth in Birmingham in 1985 Neil Kinnock was quick to attack what he described as 'tribal attitudes' of the latter, while Birmingham MP Roy Hattersley saw black behaviour as 'an act of criminal mayhem'.[1] When Mrs Thatcher's third administration began to devise its first new proposals to restrict entry to the UK Gerald Kaufman, shadow Foreign Secretary, led a delegation whose purpose it was to warn the Home Secretary, Douglas Hurd, 'not to pretend that Labour wanted to open the immigration floodgates'.[2] Britain's longstanding party-political consensus on race is, if anything, firmer than ever.

The pattern is all too familiar. During the early part of 1987 Neil Kinnock visited India and made a series of promises to the Indian government about the changes that he would make to Britain's laws concerning immigration and nationality were he to be elected Prime Minister. On his return, however, Kinnock met with Conservative criticism: it was said that he wanted to loosen immigration procedures, allow more people into the country, etc. His response? Outrage that Labour's commitment to firm immigration control had been called in question, to insist that no more people would be allowed into Britain under a Labour government than under a Conservative one and to stress that, in all this, he was only restating Labour Party policy.

With such an opposition in front of Mrs Thatcher, it is no wonder that people are pessimistic about overcoming her on race. But if we centre *our* opposition on two issues – issues that, to adopt Mrs Thatcher's phrase for a moment, are matters of 'conviction politics' – we can win the day. Those two issues are ones that I have seen as priorities since my earliest involvement with WAR: racially motivated violence and the full panoply of immigration controls.

Countering racism: a two-pronged offensive

Racist attacks and immigration controls are matters that are both immediate and far-reaching. On the one hand, time is short. Beatings multiply each year; so do forcible expulsions. On the other hand, the fight against racism is an inescapable prerequisite for broader social change. Without mass contempt for the way in which black people are treated by the authorities and individual racists, any significant repulse to the onward march of reaction in Britain is inconceivable. Indeed the establishment's broad diffusion of racism fosters an atmosphere in which every British citizen, black and white, can look forward only to more restricted democratic rights.

A real anti-racist movement will, for the first time, give the government some explaining to do. But we must be realistic. A movement that asserts that the state is the main enforcer of racism must be prepared to question what has become orthodoxy and be prepared too to be the harbinger of a new political outlook. In short, successful anti-racism will have to overturn the current consensus on race and replace it with a new one. Nothing less will do.

It will not be good enough to focus on the most extreme manifestations of racism or to ask people to be charitable towards the victims of these. Such action would ignore the permeation of racism throughout everyday life; it would leave racism intact. A new movement is an urgent project, which will not be achieved unless we make a break with the past.

If they are to win any serious support, anti-racists must answer the question 'Why should we care?' It is appalling that people are regularly killed, maimed, sacked, deported and imprisoned because of their ethnic origin: but those who see black people as competitors for jobs and housing will lose little sleep over such incidents. What needs explaining is why the defence of black people is crucial even to those poor whites who presently see blacks as rivals.

Our appeal must be not to humanitarianism but to self-interest. We propose the defence of black people not simply out of pity, and not at all out of a desire to 're-educate' the guilty, but because we are democrats. Any trend towards the restriction of black rights is bound, in the current climate, to harm the mass of the population too. We propose the defence

of black people because state-organized or state-backed oppression of black people puts the future of all civil liberties in
Britain in peril. We also propose such a defence because
racial oppression creates a poisonous atmosphere in which
'foreigners' become the enemy, not only at home but abroad
too. So long as attacks on black people are accepted, Britain's
armed forces will be able to attack targets overseas with im-
punity. Every racist murder, if left politically unchallenged,
increases the danger of another and greater massacre, such as
the sinking of the *General Belgrano*.

We live in an increasingly protectionist world economic
system – one in which the global experience of recession
opens up national antagonisms as never before. Since, as we
have seen, the seeds of racism were first sown by the nation-
state, we have no choice but to fight racism from a resolutely
anti-nationalist standpoint. Thus we must oppose immigration control not just because of the suffering it causes
but because we are proud to reject national division and
hostility and because we identify a thousand times more with
the victim of racism than with the perpetrator – the government of Britain. Again, we must counter racist attacks not
just with indignation but with the clear understanding that
each successful new attack both strengthens the trend towards repression at home and facilitates support for British
military intervention abroad. To poor whites we point out
that the Home Office 'fishing exercise' today leads to the
DHSS snoopers-versus-scroungers raid tomorrow; that the
council estate attack on Asians ends up in the Heysel stadium
massacre; that a floating prison for Tamils opens the way to
the building of more prisons for all dissenters. Britain's white
working class has a direct interest in investing its energies in
a fight against racism if it is not to be rounded up, politically
degraded and made to lose all identity and self-respect.

National chauvinism and racism are so central to British
political culture that charitable sentiments will do nothing to
dent them. What we must create is an attitude that recognizes
the practical and immediate political benefits of upholding

solidarity with the world's oppressed. Every time a British trade unionist refuses to believe what the employers, the media and the government say about immigrants and black people, so much the less likely is he or she to accept the next austerity measure. Every time we refuse to cast our potential allies as villains, we will come to know better our real adversaries. In this sense anti-racism is not separate from broader economic and social struggles. Genuine anti-racism, based on a defence of foreign people against British oppressors, is the prelude to the defence of civil liberties and economic conditions at home. By standing up to the racists, those who want to protect and extend democratic rights will be strengthened. This is the only way to eliminate racial violence.

There has never been a real campaign against immigration controls. Those half-hearted protests that have occurred have been directed not at the principle of controls but at specific pieces of legislation, such as the Nationality Act or the 1971 Immigration Act. Likewise Britain has seen a mere handful of concerted actions against racist violence, all of which have been limited in duration and in geographical scope.

This state of affairs is a disgrace. Immigration laws are nothing less than an attempt to widen the chasm between a few relatively wealthy nations and a mass of very poor ones. In effect, they are a Western message to the Third World: 'Yes, we have taken your wealth, we control your resources and we have even taken your people to work for us – but, no, we are not prepared to share any of our gains with you, for we intend forcibly to remove you whenever we wish.' In this respect Britain's immigration rules recall the pass laws of South Africa – except that they control not travel within one nation but world travel.

Although Britain's immigration controls are inevitably racist, opposition to them takes the form of a polite request for the government to implement non-racist laws.[3] But there can be no such thing as non-racist immigration laws. Why? Because the bulk of those who wish to settle in Britain come from the poor countries of the world, and those countries are without exception non-white. Thus any measures that restrict entry will, *irrespective of their wording*, in practice restrict the entry of black people. The only consistent position for opponents of racial violence is to refuse to accept all immigration legislation.

In Britain the response to racist attacks has been equally pitiful. There are worries about right-wing death squads in El Salvador, but little is said about their imitators over here. It is possible to mobilize tens of thousands of people over apartheid and hold packed rallies on Central America, but when new racist measures are enacted or petrol bombs are put through letterboxes, few people register that something has happened. The closer to home the problem is, it seems, the less willing the British are to organize against it. Where race is concerned, what happens at most is that a few intellectuals make the odd TV programme – for a specialist audience, of course.

The time for arm's-length gestures is over. Telling the victims of racial assault to stand up for themselves and calling on the police to take action over harassment are simply excuses for inaction. The real need is not for black self-defence, and even less for police intervention, but for the mobilization of white people so that they *want* actively to eradicate harassment. In this latter endeavour there have been some notable successes.

Taking action: three successful challenges to racism

In August 1982 Mr Ali, a single Bangladeshi father with three children, was one of the first Asians in Labour-controlled Tower Hamlets to be moved by the council into the all-white Glamis estate in London's notorious E1 district. The council had alerted the tenants' association in advance – but the association was then led by a racist. Weeks before Mr Ali moved in, therefore, a campaign of intimidation was launched against him. Excrement was pushed through his letterbox; the words 'No Pakis here!' were daubed on the door. On the day Mr Ali was due to move in a 'reception committee' of local residents demanded that he did no such thing. The committee was led by the leader of the tenants' association.

WAR had expected something of this kind. We turned up with Mr Ali and helped to move his furniture into the flat.[4] Then the police were called. Instead of confronting the racists the police demanded to see Mr Ali's rent book and passport, so that he could prove he had the right to move in. After a scuffle a local Community Relations Council employee, Ali Asghar, was hit.

I remember the day well. While at a conference on racism held at County Hall, I received an emergency call from WAR volunteers explaining the situation, so I took the floor of the conference to announce what was happening. To his credit Labour's Russell Profitt, then a Lewisham councillor, accompanied several WAR supporters to the scene. There, despite much experience of racially charged situations, I was shocked by the sheer venom directed against WAR activists by racists surrounding Mr Ali. We were 'Paki-lovers' and 'a disgrace to our colour'. Violence literally hung in the air.

Because it was obvious that we could not leave Mr Ali and his sons alone in his new house, three WAR volunteers offered to stay overnight in case of problems. But we could not mount an endless vigil to safeguard Mr Ali. The council seemed unwilling to offer any practical aid except for the suggestion that Mr Ali might go back to his run-down home. We knew that, somehow, we had to get local people organized in Mr Ali's defence. We immediately set about this task.

Later that summer WAR planned a march against racism running from Tower Hamlets to the TUC Conference in Brighton. We decided that, rather than go around telling everyone about Mr Ali – which might have sparked off a more united lobby of racists – we would solicit support for the march and mention Mr Ali only to those who backed it. Then, over three evenings, we canvassed every home on his 500-dwelling estate. We discovered more than 300 anti-racists. Of these thirty were invited to private meetings, first at the home of Mr Ali, then at that of local anti-racist John Rees.

We explained what had happened and asked for help. From that point onward other residents of the estate stayed overnight at Mr Ali's home and kept a round-the-clock watch on his children. A neighbour, a Jewish woman who needed no convincing of the importance of anti-racism, even went so far as to patrol the area around Mr Ali's door every night for two weeks, threatening to shoot any tormentors with her son's air rifle.

The mobilization of local people proved far more effective than that of the police. The attacks on Mr Ali stopped as rapidly as they had begun. The tenants' association was taken over by anti-racists. Today there are a number of other Bengali families living on Glamis estate, and they are not subjected to attack. The racists have become the outcasts and are now isolated from their fellow residents.

Since 1982 many black families have faced Mr Ali's predicament but have not had the support he enjoyed. Yet WAR's experience on Glamis estate should become a model for defence against racist attack. It is an approach that works because it enthuses local people and creates an atmosphere in which racial violence is not tolerated. This is something that police forces and councils have proved wholly unable to achieve.

Another case that illustrates what is possible is that of George Roucou. Originally from the Seychelles, Roucou now works in the direct labour department of Manchester City Council. He is a shop steward in his union, UCATT.

I met George on a demonstration in support of another deportee, Rose Alaso, in Leeds on 13 September 1986. At the time George had been under threat of deportation for more than two years. His legal adviser, Wythenshawe Law Centre's David Graham, had set up a campaign to oppose his deportation, but it had yet to make a real impact. It had collected about 1,500 signatures on a petition; it had received a small amount of local press coverage and the favourable attention of Manchester City Council's working party on deportations. But that was all.

Something needed to be done. Manchester WAR organizers Charles Longford and Pam Lawrence visited Roucou and his common-law wife Kim on Monday, 15 September. It was then that we first learned the nature of the Home Office case against him.

Roucou had come to Britain from the Seychelles in 1975. He held a British passport. Before taking up his present post he had worked as a hotel porter and a bus conductor. Home Office rules on residence required that Roucou send his passport to the Home Office every year. All went smoothly until 1979, when the Home Office failed to return the passport, claiming that it had never arrived. Roucou was told to apply to the Seychelles for a new passport. However, by then the Seychelles were no longer a British colony. After much difficulty Roucou eventually received a Seychelles passport in 1983. Even then immigration officials kept it from him and refused him a work permit for six months.

In August 1986 Roucou was informed that he was to be deported since he no longer had a right to stay. The argument ran that his wife's British citizenship had been the only reason for his presence in the country, that his marriage had since broken down and that therefore he had to go. This was all a fabrication. After five years in Britain Roucou had the right to permanent residence. This had been denied him only because the Home Office had lost his passport. Roucou's presence in Britain was founded on his independent desire to be here, not on his ex-wife's citizenship. Since breaking up with his wife, Roucou and Kim had lived together and raised three children. His threatened deportation would split up a family of five.

Two things were immediately clear. First, Roucou was the victim of British immigration laws. Second, as a member of a trade union Roucou might gain some support from his colleagues. The only way to secure Roucou's and Kim's future was to persuade enough council workers to give him their backing. This was not easy. Manchester's direct works department had a reputation for racism, and very few black workers were employed in it. Nevertheless, we were conscious that it was in the direct works department that we had to seek support. The Home Office is rarely moved by arguments for compassion, but it might be swayed by overwhelming evidence of solidarity with Roucou among white trade unionists.

The first requirement was to get some publicity. In Manchester city centre we held a soapbox meeting on Roucou and found local television and newspapers eager to cover his case. By the end of September most Mancunians had heard of Roucou and his plight. To up the stakes we invited a member of West Germany's Green Party to the city to speak about racism. The speaker and Roucou shared a platform, and the two were interviewed on BBC radio. Then, in November 1986, Roucou spoke at a conference on racism in Europe that WAR held in Birmingham. At the event 1,500 delegates heard his case.

With this work under our belt we approached local UCATT officials for support, as well as other council unions, including NALGO and NUPE. As a result, more than thirty union activists attended a meeting at Manchester Town Hall and resolved to call for a demonstration, in working hours, on 6 February 1987. Roucou was jubilant. At the time he pointed out, 'I have waited eighteen months for a meeting like this. At last we are going to see some action. Remember, I'm not the only one. This government is using racism to divide our movement. Fighting racism is the only way to unite us against the government.'[5] At its December 1986 meeting the Joint Shop Stewards' Committee of Manchester City Council's direct works department endorsed the stewards' previous resolution. From then on Billy Gill, the organizer of the shop stewards, and Tony Whiston, a UCATT steward, attended campaign meetings.

Gill and Whiston had to place a huge amount of faith in WAR's Charles Longford. The reason was simple: we were arguing for something that many thought impossible – a walk-out, in working hours, by white male manual workers on behalf of a black deportee. This kind of solidarity was what anti-racism had to mean in practice, and we had always known was possible. But the shop stewards' committee was not optimistic, particularly given the past unwillingness of Manchester workers to take action over more bread-and-butter issues such as wages, jobs and working conditions. However, the committee was prepared to give the exercise a go and deserves much praise for doing so.

Gill organized workplace meetings at more than fifty depots. Through these meetings, held between 16 January and 5 February 1987, Roucou or one of his supporters addressed every worker employed in Manchester's direct works department – more than 3,000 in all. In addition, more than sixty other meetings of all descriptions were called over the same short period. About 3,000 letters were sent out, and a motorcade, complete with balloons, music, speeches and leaflets, steamed through Manchester on a busy Saturday. White council workers also erected, over one of Manchester's main thoroughfares, a banner in support of Roucou.

The complicated logistics of the Roucou campaign were one problem, but gaining support for the man was far more taxing. Initially some of Roucou's backers wanted to play down the issue of immigration laws and racism and instead to emphasize that he was a trade unionist who had been badly treated. But in the campaign's very first workplace meeting one right-wing worker shattered this strategy and all the illusions upon which it was based. He stood up and spouted the most extreme racist filth that anybody could recall hearing. 'Why support blacks? They breed like rabbits!' he exclaimed, going on to urge deportation with the remark, 'What's wrong with the Seychelles? I wouldn't mind going there.'

The Roucou campaign showed that, even in the defence of a single black worker's democratic rights, *it is impossible to ignore the general argument about racism.* Racists themselves brought the issue up. The only way to win support for Roucou was to take their politics on directly. That is what we did. Every meeting turned into a polarized forum, with racists on the one side and anti-racists on the other. Workers who would probably never have spoken at, or even attended, a union meeting were getting to their feet and denouncing the racists.

Controversy was a positive benefit to the campaign. Any concessions to the racists, any attempt to avoid taking on their arguments, would have meant that those without strong opinions could have sat quietly on the fence. But early on WAR decided that at every meeting its representatives should urge a vote on whether those present should attend the demonstration on Roucou's behalf. When we did this there were very few abstentions. Manchester Council's entire workforce became politicized over the issue of Roucou and the wider threat to rights if he was deported. The racists were effectively isolated: because of the big majorities in favour of action, there was no hiding place for them. Everybody knew who they were.

On 6 February 1987, 1,500 workers left work at lunchtime to demonstrate their support for George Roucou. The demand on the placards they carried was 'NO DEPORTA-TIONS'. It was an exhilarating experience to be there. From then on nobody could argue that workers were irredeemably racist and that nothing could be done.

The shop stewards were overwhelmed with the success of the stoppage. Indeed, they made the point that, through the campaign's grass-roots approach to rank-and-file trade unionists, they had for the first time developed a real knowledge of their members. The campaign had helped strengthen their union immeasurably as a result. Thus George Roucou was not the only beneficiary of the campaign. The entire workforce had gained in decisiveness, morale and consciousness – an invaluable step forward in the climate of austerity around it. Nevertheless, Roucou was still under threat of deportation. We had to continue the campaign's momentum.

On 13 March 1987 Roucou was due to appeal against the Home Office. We set ourselves the target of mobilizing a large lobby of the hearing. Once again we organized work-place meetings and sent out thousands of letters so as to have a large number of banners from trade-union organizations on the day. In the event more than 500 people, representing fifty organizations, turned up at Aldine House, the govern-ment's immigration appeals office in Manchester.

From the start the atmosphere of the hearing seemed strange to those with experience of other deportation cases. Home Office representatives were subdued, as if they ex-pected to fail. As the hearings adjudicator noted in his state-ment, there had been 'no shortage of representations on the appellant's behalf'; indeed, 'large demonstrations' had taken place in Roucou's support. The adjudicator ended by allow-ing Roucou's appeal against deportation.

This outcome was greeted with celebration all round: after three years of nightmarish uncertainty Roucou, his wife and children were safe. But, above all else, the local political situation had been transformed. A large number of trade unionists had been mobilized to defend a black deportee – and they had won. The campaign had been an inspiration not only to all anti-racists and victims of racism but also to all those who want to resist the move towards a more re-pressive, more nationalistic Britain. George Roucou:

We had the idea of going to the unions before, but we didn't get anywhere until we got support from WAR. The housing section of NUPE was the first bit of really concrete support. Me and Charlie Longford went to the meeting and won the lot of them over. Then we went to the engineers' union, and then NALGO, and then we put pressure on UCATT. WAR also expanded the campaign to Liverpool, Birmingham, London and Bristol. They worked out a full diary for me.

Some people criticized WAR when they got involved. But I said to David Graham, 'We've been sat down here for two bloody years. This organization is prepared to do the work, and they're welcome.' We didn't have the full backing of the council or the union. But we went out and we won it. We spread the word and we shared the work. When we tested our strength we found we had more than we thought.[6]

David Graham sent us a letter of which we remain proud. In it, he pointed out:

The Adjudicator referred to public support for George as one of the reasons for that decision. Nobody could be in any doubt of that support following the major demonstration by George's fellow workers on 6 February and other events organized jointly by WAR and local union members.

The contribution made by WAR members in developing the campaign's contacts with trade unions and in the labour movement and in terms of pure hard work has been enormous and is deeply appreciated.[7]

More important than pure hard work, however, was the fact that we were prepared to take on racist ideas and to show Manchester workers that racism was not in their interests. UCATT shop steward Tony Whiston:

It was a unique situation. Even during a major dispute, like the direct works strike in 1977, you didn't get the organized meetings that we've had here to win support for George. There was a tremendous amount of interest raised and it's still going on. *Now it will be clear to people that we can achieve some success.*

I never had any illusions about racism in the workplace. It's a feature of every depot you work in. But I was taken aback and almost demoralized by some of the meetings we had. Some people said the law of the land should determine whether George should stay or not. Then there was sheer, unadulterated racism that said George was black and he should go back with the rest of them. But the most fundamental opposition was that George was an immigrant and immigrants were taking jobs. There were some very heated meetings, and there were suggestions that we should limit the campaign to the question that George is a trade unionist. But even if we had wanted to, we wouldn't have been able to. Either antagonistically or otherwise, people saw the race issue and raised it in a wider political context.

The trade union took on board a campaign which involved far more than bread-and-butter issues. Unless trade unions do this and recognize the political nature of the attacks on all of us, they won't be able to withstand government attacks. The most important thing now is to carefully consider what's been achieved. I'm very optimistic about the future. The whole issue of immigration laws should be a subject for discussion in the trade-union movement.

By fighting a deportation an atmosphere was created in which government manoeuvres of every type were seen as suspect. Such an atmosphere assists the defence of all democratic rights. Without such rights, not only black but also white workers will suffer.

The Roucou campaign was only a beginning. It shows that the rights of black people *can* be defended – but on two conditions. First, we cannot hope to skirt around racist arguments: they need to be tackled head-on, with an implacable logic that explains why whites have an interest in opposing attacks on black people. Second, it is not enough to win the arguments: *mobilizing people to give practical support* has to follow the arguments right away if racists are to be isolated in society and their ideas made illegitimate and unpopular. The case of Metso Moncrieffe and his supporters illustrates this strategy.

In 1978 Moncrieffe, 17, left his grandparents in Jamaica to join his mother in Birmingham. On arrival, he attended a college of further education, sat O-levels and began a course in electrical engineering, only to give it up because of financial problems. A keen cricketer, Moncrieffe became a member of Warwickshire County Cricket Club and was picked for the junior team.

After making a series of efforts to secure a grant for his studies, Moncrieffe was forced to leave his parent's house so that, as an independent adult, he would be more likely to qualify for finance. He moved into a room in Handsworth in Birmingham and was forced to claim social security. He got into financial difficulties and eventually grew desperate. By this time he was 21 and married; he and his wife Janet were expecting their first child.

At this point Moncrieffe succumbed to his frustrations and joined two other men in the theft of the sum of £69 from a woman coming out of a local branch of the Midland Bank.

Later in court it was acknowledged that his role in the robbery was minor, but, as he was the only one of the three men who had been caught, he was given a formidable sentence – five years.

For somebody with no previous criminal record, who had played a minor role, it was unusual for a custodial sentence to be passed, let alone one of this length. On appeal, Moncrieffe's sentence was cut to four years. The police asked for the sentence to include a deportation order, but the judge refused to recommend this, saying that the sentence alone was enough. However, on his release from prison, on 2 November 1984, Moncrieffe discovered that he had been made the subject of a deportation order.

The Home Office was categorical. It argued that the theft of £69 was a very serious offence and that, though Moncrieffe's stepfather and brothers and sister were settled here and he had been regularly visited by his mother while in prison, there was no reason why, having spent his formative years in Jamaica, he could not 'start afresh there'. The Home Office concluded: 'The Secretary of State could find no sufficient compassionate circumstances relating to the appellant which would render his exclusion undesirable.'[8]

Despite the deportation order, Moncrieffe was allowed back to Handsworth. First he lived with his parents, then he moved to his own flat. He did voluntary work with old people at a local community centre and enrolled in an electrical engineering course at Garretts Green Technical College. On 11 June 1985 police accosted Moncrieffe in the street, bundled him into the back of a van and took him to Winson Green prison, where, on Home Office orders, he was to be detained pending his removal. Moncrieffe found this experience shocking. Janet, who had already suffered a miscarriage under the stress of the deportation order, was not informed of his detention.

In July 1986 two supporters of WAR disrupted a cricket test match at Edgbaston, Birmingham, on Moncrieffe's behalf. They ran on to the pitch and unfurled a banner bearing the legend 'Metso Must Stay!'. The protest – during

which one of the participants, a woman, put two bails down
her knickers – hit the front page of all the tabloids. Next, in
October 1986, a group of Birmingham Labour councillors,
led by Phil Murphy, tried to win Moncrieffe the backing of
the Labour-dominated local authority. They were not only
turned down: for his pains Murphy found himself removed
from his post by his Labour colleagues. Finally, in December
1986, 1,000 local people marched in support of Moncrieffe.
That was the beginning of a U-turn by the Home Office.

In September 1987, more than three years after his deportation had been ordered and more than five since he was first
arrested, Moncrieffe was told he could stay. His comments:

I was tried and convicted and served my sentence. That was my
punishment. Then they tried to punish me again by deporting me.
This couldn't happen to an English person.

If it hadn't been for the fact that a campaign was fought to keep
me here, I would now be out of the country and Janet would be
here on her own. It's taken three years out of our lives. It's been
constant strain and depression. At times we had to be invisible – in
hiding for two and three months at a time. I just didn't exist. I
couldn't sign on or go to work.

I'm up to my neck in debt. What kind of system is it that tries and
convicts you, gives you a sentence a white person would never get
and then, against the judge's wishes, tries to deport you, to punish
you a second time, all for a theft of £69?[9]

Shaping the future

It should be the aim of anti-racists to build a movement
against Britain's pass laws and their violent consequences.
Our success will aid all those under Mrs Thatcher's hammer
and will help to build an opposition in a period when Her
Majesty's official one has ceased to have any credibility. To
the view that white British workers will never support the
freedom of black people to enter this country and will never
be concerned about the violence that they encounter, we
have a counter-argument that works.

Underlying acceptance of the need to control immigration is the argument that a large population is the cause of poverty and unemployment – an argument that stretches back to the writings of the Reverend Thomas Malthus. In a period of prosperity this contention has little or no consequence, but during a period of recession it accelerates the search for scapegoats. In France Algerians and Moroccans are blamed; in West Germany, Turks; in America, Hispanics. Malthusian economics are alive and well and living all over the West.

Of course the problem before society is not population size, but rather the inability of free-market economies to generate enough profit to provide new homes, services and jobs. The deportation of all of Britain's 2.5 million blacks would not change this situation. The collapse of manufacturing profitability is a phenomenon, indeed, that stretches from Ohio to Osaka. The misery it brings is the fault of the economic system, not of immigration.

Opposing immigration controls, insisting on an open-door policy, is the only guarantee that blacks will not be targeted as the culprits responsible for economic decline. It is the only stratagem that offers any hope of a real escape from contracting resources. Concession to a racist standpoint, in the form of acceptance of the need for *some* immigration controls, simply gives Mrs Thatcher and her cohorts full rein.

Would virginity or genetic tests ever be applied to white Americans? Would the British government set up special visa offices in Sydney to delay Australians in the way that Indians are delayed? There is one law for the rich and white, another for the poor and black. It is not so hard to convince white British workers of this, for it accords with much of their experience.

There are millions of white anti-racists in Britain. There are also millions of black and Asian people. The raw material for a massive anti-racist movement exists. Such a movement would have to deal with the issues that this book raises. A mass anti-racist movement, we repeat, is needed as much by white working class people as it is by blacks. The government and its various agencies will not fight racism. An effective anti-racist movement must be based on large numbers of people regularly organizing action against racist violence and racist laws; it cannot be a top-heavy campaign for pressurizing prominent personalities through the 'normal channels'. It must be a radical movement for the defence and extension of rights, and it must be entirely independent of national or local government. Its funds should come from donations from anti-racists. In addition to campaigning it will have to offer practical assistance to the victims of racial violence, immigration laws, police harassment, legal injustice and racial discrimination.

No anti-racist movement can be successful unless it moves large numbers of white people to oppose racial violence. Only then will we be able to break up, once and for all, the racist consensus created over the past thirty years. In Appendix 1 we present a manifesto that, we believe, can form the basis for a mass campaign against racism. Once this, or something like it, has been widely adopted, there will be a new beginning in this country. When millions of ordinary British people begin to repudiate the daily diet of nationalism with which they are now presented, life will be very different.

Postscript

Under Siege is both a warning and a solution. We have shown the scale of racism and the impact that it has on those who suffer its consequences. We have also argued that only the foolish can afford to be indifferent to racial violence. If racial hatred spreads and intensifies it will claim many victims – of all colours.

In this sense a genuine movement against racism cannot be merely a 'single-issue' campaign. It will be an unmistakeable challenge to the worst aspects of the British way of life. Here it would be as well to register our disagreement with the Labour Party notion that people in their millions have been won across to Mrs Thatcher's ideas. In our view, millions of working-class people have deserted Labour not because they have become Conservatives but because they have yet to be provided with a credible opposition to Mrs Thatcher, one that does not feel awkward about standing up for the poor and the oppressed.

We are well into a period in which the consensus politics of the prosperous 1960s has given way to polarization and division. The political solutions of the past are not relevant to the future. Labour's demise and the paralysis of the other political parties are acute signs of this. The fight to end racism is a fight for unity in the midst of fragmentation and for a new kind of politics that fits the needs of our times. It is a fight for our survival against those who would prefer us to fight each other. We have said that the stakes are high; indeed, we believe that the future of mankind itself is at stake. Yet we are confident that a genuine anti-racism will irrevocably set its stamp on Britain before the millennium is out.

Appendix 1

Manifesto for an anti-racist movement

A 1,500-strong conference held in Birmingham in November 1986 passed the following manifesto as the basis on which a European-wide anti-racist movement can be created. The conference, initiated by Workers Against Racism, was attended by representatives from scores of anti-racist and immigrant organizations from Britain and Europe. It also had representatives from a wide spectrum of political opinion, including a delegation from West Germany's Greens.

Please ask your own organization to discuss and adopt this manifesto, and let us know of your support. If you would like to contact WAR, please telephone us on (01)-729 0414.

THE BIRMINGHAM MANIFESTO

Racism is on the rise throughout Europe. Public hostility against immigrants, refugees from the Third World and black people in general has reached unprecedented proportions. Among European governments it is now the done thing to promote an aggressive xenophobia. Politicians and the media work together to create a climate of opinion in which racism is allowed to flourish.

One government after another puts through new immigration regulations and fresh internal controls over the activities of immigrants and black people. New legislation is backed by a propaganda barrage which seeks to target foreigners as objects of suspicion, or even of hatred. The policy of labelling foreigners as a potential menace to society allows the security forces to stop, search and question anybody whose face does not fit in a crowd of respectable white Europeans. In London, Paris and Berlin, only the language is different: the message that non-Europeans are not welcome is the same.

All the signs suggest, however, that the anti-immigrant drive is only in its early stages. The emergency conference against terrorism, attended by EEC Home Affairs ministers in London at the end of September 1986, gave an indication of the way things are moving. All European governments have taken advantage of the panic about terrorism to tighten up supervision over border crossings, step up the public profile of the military and to invoke the need for more repressive measures.

Criminalization

Officially sponsored campaigns against narcotics, crime, prostitution and immorality generally incorporate a more or less openly racist theme. Blacks are blamed for peddling drugs, muggings, turning respectable areas into red-light districts, and for transmitting AIDS from Africa. Public scares around these issues are used to justify police raids, mass arrests and tough sentences, as well as stricter controls on immigration. They also provoke physical attacks on ethnic minorities by white racists.

Labelling all blacks and foreigners as potential criminals is a key aspect of the racist campaign. All European governments have made law and order a central theme of official policy. Artificially created panics distract attention from the problems of industrial decline and mass unemployment and help to consolidate public opinion in defence of the existing order.

The rulers of the major European nations aim to foster an atmosphere of fear and insecurity in which all classes will rally together against imagined threats to stability. Their object is to encourage people to forget about the difficulties of finding or holding down a decent job; instead they urge people to stand together against alien evils. They want to turn immigrants and blacks into scapegoats for the failures of their economic and political system.

Our response

Until now it has been the racists who have monopolized political discussion in Europe. Though many people are disgusted with the anti-foreign stance of politicians and just as many loathe the racist features and cartoons that fill the popular press, anti-racists have for the most part been disorientated by the ferocity of the racist offensive, if not corrupted by the pull of state institutions. Many, too, have remained largely inactive.

As a result of these developments, immigrants and black people are isolated from the rest of society and are generally forced to defend themselves alone. But it is an urgent necessity to change this state of affairs. The growth of racism must be countered by an anti-racist movement that links up every European country. We need a movement that is not prepared to make the slightest concession to racism in any of its manifestations – one that is ready to act against racism, not just sigh about it. Such a movement can be built around the following principles.

* No to all racist laws!

Laws which discriminate against immigrants help to establish a framework for the policies of divide and rule. It is vital that anti-racists oppose immigration controls in any form. Equally, everybody who lives in Britain should have the same rights, irrespective of their national or ethnic origin. Another key point is that all forms of 'ethnic monitoring' by the state must be opposed. Information gathered in this way can only be to the detriment of black people and immigrants.

* Full rights for refugees!

European governments must be forced to take full responsibility for refugees fleeing Western-sponsored oppression in the Third World. Refugees should be granted full civil rights, in whichever country they choose to settle in.

* Stop police repression!

It is essential to stand up against the criminalization of black people. The identification of blacks with crime strengthens the prejudice that immigrants are the central problem facing society. Our aim should be to turn people's anger against the real cause of poverty and their sufferings – the free-market capitalist system. Those falsely imprisoned, as in the case of the Broadwater Farm trial victims, should be released at once. They are nothing less than political prisoners – the victims of the racist offensive.

* *Resist racial violence!*

The state cannot be relied upon to combat racial violence. On the contrary, the policies of every state in Europe have helped to make racism respectable. The only way to deal with racist violence is to mobilize direct action by workers and anti-racists. It is the responsibility of anti-racists to organize political and, where necessary, physical support for those on the receiving end of racial oppression.

* *Co-ordinated international action*

Although racism has distinct national features, it is a danger that threatens every country in Europe. To meet this danger effectively requires the active co-operation of anti-racists throughout the continent.

Appendix 2
Statistical information

In writing *Under Siege* it became apparent that there were no easily available statistical data on Britain's black community or even simple information about immigration and racial violence. This appendix by no means supplies all that is needed, but it does give some idea of the history of immigration.

A word of warning is required. Many anti-racists have attempted to substitute statistics for argument when opposing racism. Tables 1 and 2, for example, show quite clearly that the population of Britain has declined by about 500,000 since 1951: in other words, emigration has more than offset immigration. A fact such as this, however, does little to convince racists that their concern about 'swamping' is irrational, although in the 1970s the Anti-Nazi League and the Socialist Workers Party thought that it did. A pamphlet entitled 'The Case Against Immigration', published by the Socialist Workers Party in 1978, argued:

41,500 more people *left* the United Kingdom than entered it in 1976–77. And who were the immigrants? The largest group – 22,000 – came from Australia, followed by 21,000 from the Common Market countries and 16,000 from the African Commonwealth. Two other statistics are interesting. In 1976–77 slightly more West Indians *left* the country than entered it. Moreover, there was a net inflow of 200 immigrants from South Africa.

Many black people will feel that it is insulting and degrading to them even for socialists to argue about the immigration and birth-rate figures in the way we have done. Why shouldn't black people enter the country freely and have as many children as they want? It is, none the less, important to let people have the facts on the issue.[1]

Despite the noble intentions of this argument it concedes ground to racism. For the ordinary reader it implies that immigration would be a problem only if there were large numbers entering the country. It invites a counter-argument: 'All very well, but a complete end to immigration would still help our economy, which can't afford the slightest extra strain.' It fails to acknowledge that for a racist housed in a predominantly black ghetto a surplus of emigration over immigration does not change the fact that black people are 'swamping' the area. It also neglects another fact – that when the overall population shrinks it is likely that a higher proportion of those remaining will be black. Black people represented 0.4 per cent of Britain's population in 1951, 1 per cent in 1961, 2.3 per cent in 1971 and 3.9 per cent in 1981; they constituted 4.3 per cent of the population in 1987 (see Figure 9).

Racism cannot be fought by playing the numbers game. Statistics cannot replace the need to argue that the defence of the rights of black people is in the direct and immediate interests of all ordinary people in Britain.

Immigration and emigration, 1951–81

Table 1

Decade	Population change due to immigration and emigration
1951–61	+ 12,000
1961–71	− 320,000
1971–81	− 391,000
Total	− 699,000

Source: Office of Population and Census Surveys, 1982.

Figure 1

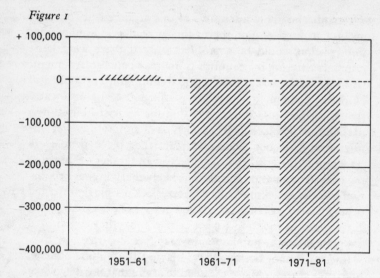

Source: Office of Population and Census Surveys, 1982.

Migration to and from Britain, 1972–83

Table 2

Year	Population change due to immigration and emigration
1972	− 11,000
1973	− 50,000
1974	− 85,000
1975	− 41,000
1976	− 19,000
1977	− 46,000
1978	− 5,000
1979	+ 6,000
1980	− 55,000
1981	− 79,000
1982	− 57,000
1983	+ 17,000
Total	− 430,000

Source: Office of Population and Census Surveys, Population Trends series, 1984.

Figure 2

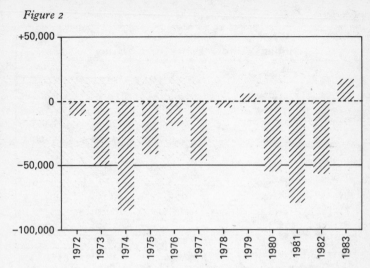

Source: Office of Population and Census Surveys, Population Trends series, 1984.

Immigration from the New Commonwealth, 1953–62

Table 3 and Figure 3 show the pattern of New Commonwealth immigration following the Second World War. Until 1953 there was virtually no immigration. From that date the first Afro-Caribbean immigrants began to arrive, followed by Asians a couple of years later. By 1962 there was a large increase in numbers, partly because the 1962 Commonwealth Immigrants Act raised fears in the Third World that families already partly settled in Britain would not be able to bring in relatives.

Table 3

Year	West Indians	Indians	Pakistanis	Others	Total
1953	2,000				2,000
1954	11,000				11,000
1955	27,500	5,800	1,850	7,500	42,650
1956	29,800	5,600	2,050	9,350	46,800
1957	23,000	6,600	5,200	7,600	42,400
1958	15,000	6,200	4,700	3,950	29,850
1959	16,400	2,950	850	1,400	21,600
1960	49,650	5,900	2,500	−350	57,700
1961	66,300	23,750	25,100	21,250	136,400
*1962	31,800	19,050	25,080	18,970	94,900
Total	272,450	75,840	67,330	69,670	485,300

Source: Z. Leyton Henry, *The Politics of Race in Britain*, 1984.
Note: *The figures for 1962 apply only to the first six months of that year, before the new Act became operative.

Figure 3

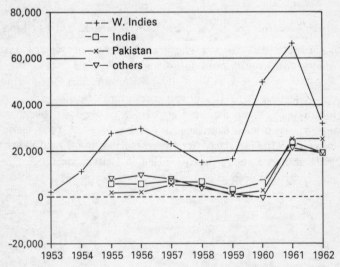

Source: Z. Leyton Henry, *The Politics of Race in Britain*, 1984.

The replacement of primary by secondary immigration, 1963–71

Table 4 and Figure 4 illustrate the impact of initial first post-war statutes on immigration – statutes that prevented entry to the UK unless the entrant had a voucher for work. The overall effect was to put a stop to primary immigration and to restrict immigration to the dependants of those already here. By the time of the 1971 Immigration Act entrants from the New Commonwealth ran at half the 1962 figure and were declining.

Table 4

Year	Voucher holders	Dependants	Total*
1963	28,678	24,459	56,071
1964	13,888	35,738	52,840
1965	12,125	39,228	53,650
1966	5,141	39,130	46,602
1967	4,716	50,083	57,648
1968	4,353	42,036	50,160
1969	3,512	27,984	33,942
1970	3,052	21,337	26,562
1971	2,407	18,712	23,611

Source: Home Office statistics, extracted in Runnymede Trust Statistical Bulletin, 1973.
Note: * The figure in the total column is greater than the sum of the other two because it includes those who were neither dependants nor voucher holders.

Figure 4

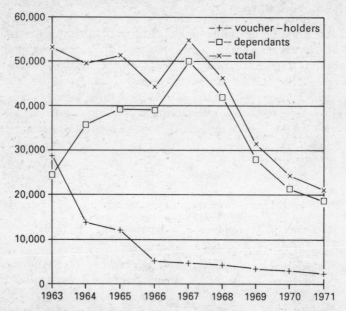

Source: Home Office statistics, extracted in Runnymede Trust Statistical Bulletin, 1973.

Immigration from the New Commonwealth and Pakistan since 1953

Figure 5 shows that the trend of immigration has been markedly downwards with the exception of the years directly before a new piece of legislation has become operative. Since the Nationality Act took effect in 1983 the trend has again been sharply downwards. The new legislation proposed for 1988–89 will accelerate this trend.

Figure 5

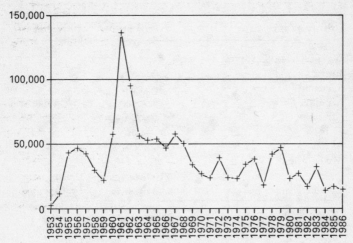

Source: CRE, *Immigration Control Procedures Investigation*, 1985, and Labour Research, November 1987.

Britain's ethnic minorities: size and proportion born in Britain

We now turn to the current composition of Britain's ethnic minority in terms of overall numbers and the percentage of these born here. Altogether getting on for half Britain's 'immigrants' are native to the UK.

Table 5

Ethnic group	Number	Percentage born here
W. Indian and Guyanese	530,000	54
Indian	760,000	43
Pakistani	380,000	42
Bangladeshi	90,000	31
African	100,000	35
Chinese	110,000	20
Arab	60,000	10
Mixed origin	210,000	75
Other	100,000	25
Total	2,340,000	40

Source: *Survey of Current Affairs*, HMSO, February 1987.

Figure 6

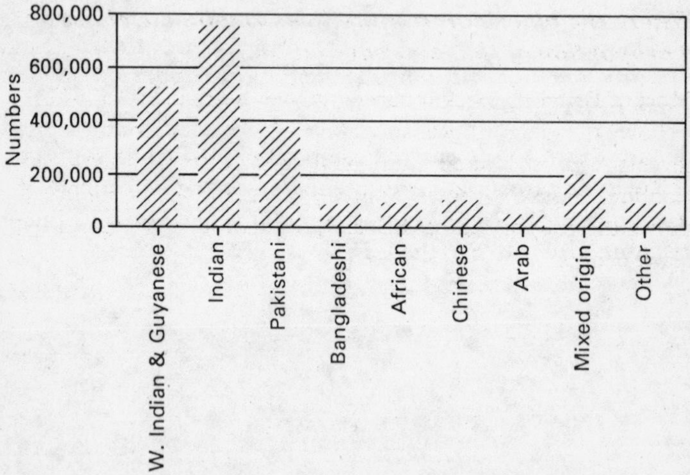

Source: *Survey of Current Affairs*, HMSO, February 1987.

Figure 7

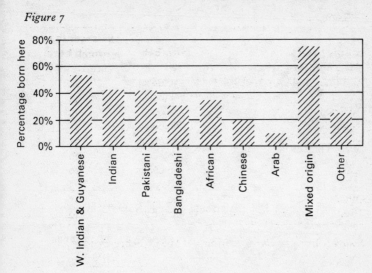

Source: *Survey of Current Affairs*, HMSO, February 1987.

Where the black community lives and its numbers as a proportion of the total population

Most of Britain's black inhabitants live in urban areas. Table 6 shows the geographical spread of the black community and reveals why so much municipal anti-racism is based in London. Figure 8 shows Table 6 in graphic form; Figure 9 shows the proportion of the total population represented by black people.

Table 6

Metropolitan area	Numbers	Percentage of national black community
London (inner and outer)	914,000	39.06
West Midlands	372,000	15.90
Greater Manchester	143,000	6.11
West Yorkshire	118,000	5.04
Other areas	793,000	33.89
Total	2,340,000	100.00

Source: Office of Population and Census Surveys, *Monitor*, December 1986.

Figure 8

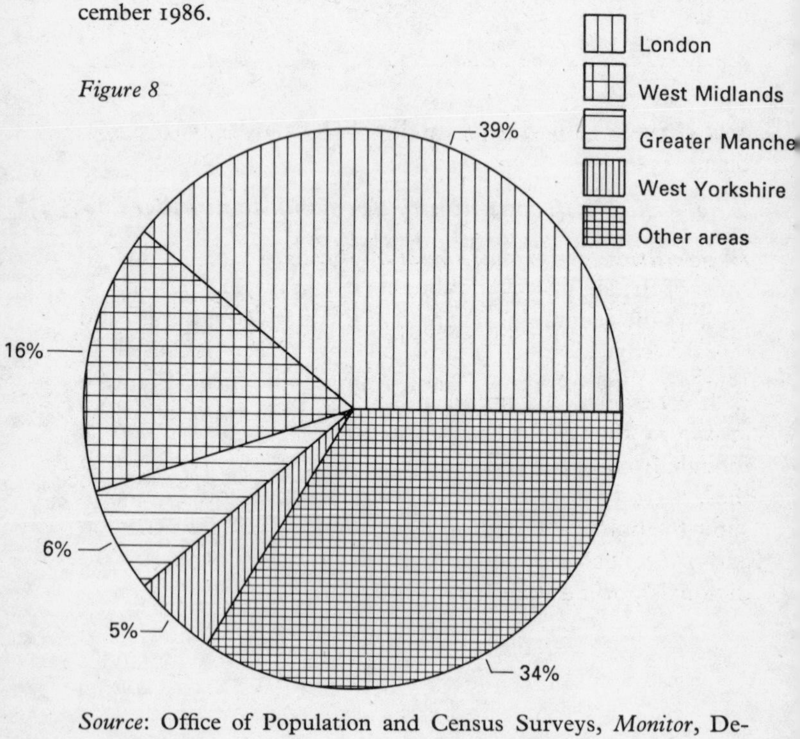

Source: Office of Population and Census Surveys, *Monitor*, December 1986.

Figure 9

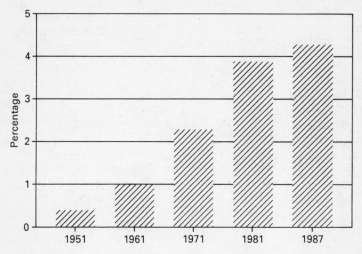

Source: Office of Population and Census Surveys, *Monitor*, December 1986.

Deportation orders and racist murders

At first sight the last two tables and figures appear unconnected, but on closer inspection their similarity is striking. A surge in the number of deportations is strongly correlated with a surge in the number of racist killings. Figures for *attempted* killings for the period 1970–85 are not available, though from experience in east London I would say that these were the most horrific years. Table 7 and Figure 10 show the number of deportation orders issued between 1973 and 1982, Table 8 and Figure 11, racist killings (by individuals), over a slightly longer period.

Table 7

Year	Number of deportation orders issued
1973	465
1974	427
1975	545
1976	789
1977	1,157
1978	1,234
1979	1,275
1980	2,472
1981	2,195
1982	1,986
Total	12,545

Source: Home Office Statistics Bulletin, H M S O, 1983.

Figure 10

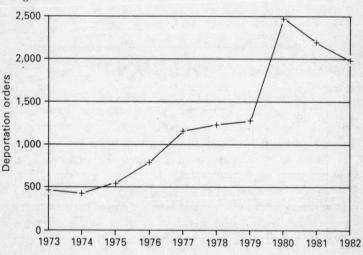

Source: Home Office Statistics Bulletin, H M S O, 1983.

Table 8

Year	Number of racist murders
1970	2
1971	1
1972	0
1973	3
1974	0
1975	2
1976	5
1977	0
1978	8
1979	3
1980	6
1981	26
1982	0
1983	0
1984	1
1985	6
Total	63

Source: Paul Gordon, *Runnymede Trust Survey*, 1986.

Figure 11

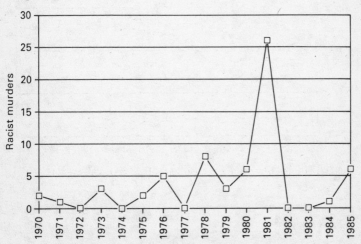

Source: Paul Gordon, *Runnymede Trust Survey*, 1986.

Notes and references

Introduction

1. *Daily Mirror*, 21 August 1980.

2. Interview with Pam Lawrence of Manchester WAR, September 1987.

3. *Guardian*, 16 February 1988, p.7.

4. ibid.

5. Home Office, *Racial Attacks*, 1981.

1   The public and racial violence

1. Metropolitan Police Community Relations Branch, *Racial Harassment Action Guide*, January 1987, pp. 6 – 9.

2. *Independent*, 2 February 1987.

3. Letter from Nasreen to Lewis, 7 March 1982.

4. Letter from Lewis to Nasreen, 23 March 1982.

5. Letter from Nasreen to Lewis, 27 March 1982.

6. Letter from Lewis to Nasreen, 3 April 1982.

7. Letter from Banks to Nasreen, 9 April 1984.

8. Letter from Banks to Nasreen, 30 March 1985.

9. Letter from C. D. Inge, Home Office, to Nasreen, 11 February 1983.

10. Letter from Chief Superintendent Barrett, West Ham police, to Banks, 13 February 1985.

11. Letter from Newham Council to Banks, 15 February 1985.

12. Ezaz Hayat, speaking to a member of ELWAR, 12 December 1986.

13. Interview with E L W A R, 12 December 1986.

14. For legal reasons false names have been inserted here.

15. Statement of Dalton Macauley, 15 October 1986.

16. Statement of Dalton Macauley to the police, 7 November 1986.

17. Interview with E L W A R, 12 August 1987.

18. ibid.

19. ibid.

20. Metropolitan Police, *Racial Harassment Action Guide*, January 1987.

2 Institutional harassment

1. Cited in *Policing London*, No. 4, November 1982, p. 1.

2. ibid.

3. *Daily Mirror*, 30 June 1982. The journalist, Bruce Porter, is a respected ex-*Newsweek* man: he taped Newman's remarks only to have their existence officially denied.

4. *Caribbean Times*, 28 August 1987, p. 5.

5. *Daily Express*, 6 November 1987.

6. London Weekend Television broadcast, 11 July 1986.

7. *Sunday Times*, 22 February 1987.

8. ibid.

9. Eyewitness to the killing of Clinton McCurbin, quoted in the *Guardian*, 23 February 1987.

10. *The Times*, 27 February 1987.

11. *Wolverhampton Express and Star*, 6 March 1987, p. 1.

12. *Guardian*, 1 February 1988, p. 2.

13. *Economist*, 2 July 1983.

14. Thanks are due to the Monerville family, in particular Annette and John Monerville, for their co-operation in the writing of this section.

15. *Guardian*, 19 January 1987.

16. Interview with W A R, 15 January 1987.

17. Inspector Terence Walters, letter to Hackney and Stoke Newington community groups, 31 March 1987.

18. Hansard, 22 October 1986.

19. Inspector Basil Griffiths, deputy chair of the Police Federation, speech to the Conservative Party Monday Club, quoted in *The Times*, 7 October 1982.

20. Police Federation spokesman, *Guardian*, 20 November 1982.

21. Middlesbrough home-beat officer P C Hudson was caught handing out a leaflet headed 'Questionnaire for Employment' (minorities division). It caused a sensation in the local press (see *Middlesbrough Evening Gazette*, 1 March 1987). Leaflet kindly lent by Abdul Choudhray, Westlane, Middlesbrough.

22. Thanks are due to John Fitzpatrick and Beverley Brown of Hammersmith Law Centre for their co-operation.

23. Interview with W A R, September 1987.

24. Report of trial by a supporter of W A R.

25. *The Times*, 17 June 1987.

26. Interview with W A R, February 1987.

27. *Sun*, 22 May 1987, p. 24.

28. *New Statesman*, 26 February 1988, p. 3.

29. Records of Tottenham magistrates' court, December 1985.

30. What follows is taken from the coroner's court record of the inquest into the death of Mrs Cynthia Jarrett.

31. Coroner's comment in the record of the inquest into the death of Mrs Cynthia Jarrett, Tottenham coroner's court, 1985.

32. ibid.

33. The officers claim to have knocked before entering, but none could remember the type of door knocker on the door. D C Randall, who says he did the knocking, described it entirely wrongly in his evidence.

34. Record of the inquest evidence, op. cit.

35. ibid.

36. *Mail on Sunday*, 6 October 1985.

37. Lord Gifford, Q C, *et al.*, *The Broadwater Farm Inquiry*, London, 1986, p. 89.

38. ibid., p. 95.

39. ibid., p. 111.

40. Interview with WAR, 20 March 1987.

41. *The Broadwater Farm Inquiry*, op. cit., p. 120.

42. After the previous weekend, when there had been fighting in Brixton following the police shooting of Cherry Groce, the *Guardian* reported, 'There was a large contingent from the Revolutionary Communist Party (RCP), which, like other extremist groups present, appeared to be doing its best to revive enthusiasm for attacking the police verbally or physically when the violence was in fear of flagging.' The RCP denied this, while emphasizing its support for black youth resisting police attacks. Then, after Tottenham, Sir Kenneth Newman told a press conference at Scotland Yard that groups of Trotskyists and anarchists, black and white, orchestrated the disturbances in both Tottenham and Brixton. Indeed, the *Daily Express* reported that 'street-fighting experts trained in Moscow and Libya' were behind the uprisings. By 17 October, however, Scotland Yard recanted on Broadwater Farm. A statement declared, 'No evidence of agitation before the riot by politically inspired groups has been found by police. We don't believe outside agitators were responsible for what happened.'

43. *The Broadwater Farm Inquiry*, op. cit., p. 133.

44. Report by the Broadwater Farm Youth Association into the trials of those arrested, October 1987.

45. Interview with WAR, cited in *The Next Step*, 20 March 1987, p. 1.

46. Interview with Peter Kane of the *Daily Mirror*. Kane was handed documents about the case found on a rubbish tip in east London: he reported their contents in the *Daily Mirror* , 19 October 1987.

47. Margaret Burnham, *Draft Report of International Observers at the Broadwater Farm Trial*, pp. 9 –10.

3   Racism: roots and development

1. Paul Gordon, *Racial Violence and Harassment*, Runnymede Trust Research Report, March 1986, p. 36.

2. Even the left was imbued with the colonial mentality. In 1933

the Labour Party document *The Colonies*, Policy Report No. 6, stated: 'There are territories, for example, in the West Indies, where people are probably already capable of managing their own affairs. There is no reason why they should not be given a large measure of self-government. On the other hand, the African territories are, in this respect, entirely different. Their people are in a condition which would make it impossible for them to take over the government of their country on modern lines. In such cases what is required is education and preparation with the definite object of training the population in self-government.' The Labour left was particularly open about its allegiance to Empire. In 1947, in its manifesto *Keep Left*, it encouraged Labour Prime Minister Clement Attlee to strengthen Britain's grip on the Third World: 'Once we give up the attempt to hold the Middle East by force, we can concentrate our manpower and resources on the African development which should be our main colonial responsibility in the next thirty years . . . It is not an exaggeration to say that the future of European socialism depends on the success of our combined colonial policies in the African continent.' *Tribune*, the leading paper of the Labour left, declared a year later: 'We do not need to apologize for our mission in Africa. Whatever the reasons which took our forbears there we must stay,' (20 August 1948).

3. The career of Thomas Carlyle illustrates this development. In his youth Carlyle was a courageous critic of British society and a passionate reformer in the best traditions of the nascent bourgeoisie. However, the European revolutions of 1848 prompted him to rethink his position. Threats to political stability made Carlyle acutely aware of the danger of the masses to his peers: he therefore decided to put his considerable talents as a publicist to use on the latter's behalf. Carlyle glorified the English race and justified Britain's oppression of inferior people by arguing that they were appointed by God to serve his country. See Peter Fryer, *Staying Power*, Pluto Press, London, 1988, who describes this period in considerable detail.

4. Fryer, op. cit.

5. Karl Marx, writing at the time, noted this: 'The English bourgeoisie has not only exploited the Irish poverty to keep down the working class in England by forced immigration of poor Irishmen, but it has also divided the proletariat into two hostile camps. The English worker hates the Irish worker as a competitor who lowers

wages and the standard of life. He feels national and religious antipathies for him. He regards him somewhat like the poor whites of the Southern states of North America regard their black slaves. This antagonism among the proletarians of England is artificially nourished and supported by the bourgeoisie. It knows this scissor is the true secret of maintaining its power' (Marx and Engels, *Ireland and the Irish Question*, Progress Publishers, Moscow, 1978). The parallel that Marx drew between black people in America and the Irish in Britain was not an arbitrary one. Racism unites people of different skin colour in a common experience – that of oppression.

6. Peter Fryer, *New Statesman*, 4 December 1987, p. 29.

7. ibid.

8. Quoted in Commission for Racial Equality, *Immigration Control Procedures: Report of a Formal Investigation*, London, 1985, p. 13.

9. Cabinet Foreign Labour Committee, Minutes, 14 March 1946.

10. Hansard, 8 June 1948.

11. Cabinet Papers, 1951.

12. Cabinet Papers, 1954.

13. ibid.

14. Maxwell-Fyfe reported to the Cabinet on the immigration figures of his day and concluded: 'These figures do not seem to me to justify any departure from the view which has hitherto been taken that so far no such evil consequences of this immigration have appeared as would amount to a case for legislation directed against the immigration of British subjects, with all the political and administrative difficulties to which it would give rise' (Cabinet Papers, 1954).

15. ibid.

16. ibid.

17. *South London Press*, 28 January 1955.

18. Hansard, 5 December 1958.

19. They were Albert Evans (Islington South), Eric Fletcher (Islington East), B. J. Parker (Paddington North), W. Gibson (Clapham) and Marcus Lipton (Brixton).

20. *Kensington News*, 5 September 1958.

21. *Daily Express*, 15 November 1961.

22. Cited in *The Roots of Racism*, Junius Publications, London, 1985, p. 39.

23. Hansard, 24 March 1965.

24. Hansard, 17 November 1964, Col. 290.

25. Richard Crossman, *The Diaries of a Cabinet Minister*, Volume 1, Hamish Hamilton and Jonathan Cape, London, 1975.

26. ibid.

27. *The Times*, 1 March 1968.

28. *Daily Express*, 19 May 1976.

29. Incidentally, this, rather than the mythical success of the Anti-Nazi League in discrediting the National Front's policies, is the explanation for the present decline of the far right in British politics.

30. *World in Action*, 30 January 1978.

31. *The Times*, 16 February 1978.

32. Harry Pollitt, *Looking Ahead*, Communist Party of Great Britain publication, 1947.

33. *Guardian*, 11 July 1957.

34. *Coventry Evening Telegraph*, 5 November 1958.

35. *Coventry Evening Telegraph*, 21 October 1961.

36. *Telegraph and Argus*, 27 July 1961.

37. Interview with Radio Leicester quoted in *Race Today*, October 1974.

38. *Race Today*, September 1974.

39. TUC Hotel and Catering Industry Committee, Minutes, 19 July 1978.

40. *Guardian*, 5 May 1979.

41. Interview with Ford Dagenham foundry worker. Anonymity preserved to protect against victimization.

42. Conservative Central Office, *Conservative Party Manifesto*, 1979.

43. *Financial Times*, 31 May 1985.

44. *Sun*, 29 May 1985.

45. *Daily Telegraph*, 30 May 1985.

46. Anne Owers, 'Servants lead masters astray', *Guardian*, 8 September 1986.

47. *London Evening Standard*, 14 October 1986.

48. *Daily Mail*, 15 October 1986.

49. *Sun*, 15 October 1986.

50. *Control of Immigration Statistics*, 1082, Cmnd 8944, HMSO, 1983.

51. See *The Next Step*, 2 May 1986.

52. *Hackney Gazette*, 17 October 1986; *New Life*, 24 October 1986.

53. *City Limits*, 6 November 1986.

54. Home Office press release, 4 October 1972.

55. *The Next Step*, 11 April 1986.

56. DHSS, 'Gatecrashers', 3 October 1979.

57. Quoted in Paul Gordon, *Policing Immigration*, Pluto Press, 1982, p. 80.

58. Hansard, 17 November 1983.

59. Hansard, 2 April 1980.

60. *Guardian*, 31 October 1981.

61. *Guardian*, 29 May 1981.

62. *Daily Mail*, 28 April 1978.

63. Although a vote for strike action was taken, only twenty-six out of 111 job centres affected voted to strike. Of these twenty-five were in London; only one, in Liverpool, was outside the capital. The ethnic monitoring went ahead.

64. Colin Brown, *Black and White Britain: The Third PSI Survey*, Policy Studies Institute, London, 1984, p. 316–17.

65. PSI, 1985, and ibid.

66. *Labour Research*, May 1986.

67. House of Commons Employment Committee, *Discrimination in Employment*, session 1986–87, HMSO, 1987.

68. John Brennan and Philip McGeevor, *Employment of Graduates from Ethnic Minorities*, CRE, 1987.

69. 'Ethnic origin and employment status', *Employment Gazette*, January 1987.

70. Spitalfields Housing and Planning Rights Service, *Bengalis and GLC Housing Allocation in E1*, 1982.

71. ibid.

72. Colin Brown, *Black and White Britain*, p. 318.

73. *Race and Mortgage Lending*, CRE, 1985.

74. Muhammed Anwar and Ameer Ali, *Overseas Doctors: Experience and Expectations*, CRE, 1987.

75. *Ethnic Origin of Nurses Applying for and in Training*, CRE, 1987.

76. *No Alibi, No Excuse*, Greater London Action for Racial Equality, 1987.

77. *Daily Mail*, 11 March 1982.

78. *Guardian*, 26 July 1986.

79. *Guardian*, 30 August 1986.

4   The official opponents of racism

1. Hansard, 23 March 1965, cols. 378–85.

2. Lord Scarman, *The Scarman Report*, Penguin, Harmondsworth, 1982.

3. 'A good knight's solution', *Sunday Times*, 10 October 1982.

4. ibid.

5. *Independent*, 5 October 1987.

6. *The Roots of Racism*, Junius Publications, London, 1985, p. 51.

7. House of Commons Home Affairs Committee, *Commission for Racial Equality*, HC 46-1, HMSO, 1981.

8. *The Scarman Report*. The report has had a seminal impact on the British race-relations scene. It urged for the institutionalization of black radicals in a network of committees and monitoring projects. It was welcomed by the right for its condemnation of the rioters and by a naive left for its acceptance that the roots of the riots were in the alienation of black youth from society. The left's main criticism of the report was not of its substance but rather of the slow pace by which it was adopted by government at national and local level. Scarman's achievement was to win support for conciliation from angry black activists.

9. National Council for Voluntary Organizations, Information Sheet No. 27, January 1987.

10. For three years each time Section 11 pays 75 per cent of the salaries of those employed on approved schemes. It thus brings revenue to councils operating such schemes. One result of this is that councils provide the Home Office with regular statistics on the racial make-up of their workforces as well as the ethnic mix of users of their Section 11 schemes.

11. Section 11 money won by the London borough of Hackney rose from £50,727 to £1,533,243 in the three years following the street fighting of 1981, while that allocated to Tower Hamlets leapt from £102,989 to £1,243,946. Both Camden and Islington received windfalls of more than 400 per cent over the same period. Southwark sustained an increase of more than 300 per cent, while Brent and Lambeth more than doubled their share. Hansard, 17 May 1985.

12. As part of the Task Force project, government ministers and City financiers have worked together to set up a new enterprise agency to finance black business. It is run by Winston Collymore, the director of an 'ethnic greetings card' company and, until 1986, principal economic development officer for Haringey Council in London. Collymore's philosophy is that discrimination is unavoidable, but if more black business is created, there will be more black jobs. He at least is convinced by the government's rhetoric.

13. For example, Linford Dennis, Earl Smith and Byron Morgan run a clothing shop in Handsworth's Villa Road. The shop is funded through the Handsworth Employment Scheme. 'There's no trouble finding a workforce,' says Linford. 'Every day there's people coming around for a job. Unemployment in Handsworth is not just high, it's ridiculous, crazy.' Interview with the *Guardian*, cited in *The Next Step*, 25 September 1987.

14. House of Commons Home Affairs Committee, *Racial Disadvantage*, HC 24, HMSO, 1981.

15. ibid.

16. Herman Ousley, 'Local Authority Race Initiatives', in Martin Body and Colin Fudge, *Local Socialism*, Macmillan, London, 1984.

17. In its final year the GLC financed the two most important political campaigns in Newham – the Newham 7 Campaign (£5,800) and the Justice for the Pryces (£9,000). The Hackney Anti-

deportation Campaign received £8,700; the Turkish Solidarity Campaign, £19,673. Among many other campaigns in receipt of GLC largesse were the Mark Ponambalam campaign (£4,776), the Tamil Refugee Action Group (£6,000), the Refugee Forum (£3,010) and the Campaign Against Racism and Fascism (£18,903). See GLC Ethnic Minority Committee, *Grants Approved for 1985–86*, 1985.

18. City of Bradford Metropolitan Council Policy Unit, *Race Relations in Bradford: The Council's Approach*, 1985.

19. A. Sivanandan, 'From Resistance to Rebellion', *Race and Class*, Autumn 1981/Winter 1982.

20. A. Sivanandan, 'Challenging Racism', *Race and Class*, Autumn 1983.

21. Stafford Scott, quoted in Steve Platt, 'Return to Broadwater Farm', *New Socialist*, April 1986.

22. Even before the GLC's consultation exercise, County Hall money was channelled to selected black organizations. On taking power in 1981 the new Labour administration approved a number of black projects. Then, as soon as the Ethnic Minority Unit's parent, the Ethnic Minority Committee, was established, it allocated £895,000 in grants over the financial year 1982–83. By January 1983, 101 black groups had received monies worth 15 per cent of all the grants made by the GLC in that period. See GLC Ethnic Minorities Unit, 'Achievements', September 1983.

23. National Council for Voluntary Organizations, *After Abolition: A Report on the Impact of the Abolition of the MCCs and the GLC on the Voluntary Sector*, NCVO, 1986.

24. ibid.

25. GLC Ethnic Minorities Committee, *The GLC's Work to Assist Ethnic Minorities*, 1983.

26. GLC Ethnic Minorities Committee, *Grants Approved for 1985–86*, 1985.

27. ibid.

28. Who distributes these funds? The Race Relations Committee on which these groups' cooptees themselves sit. Thus not only are 'independent' black representatives on the council payroll but they are responsible for perpetuating this system.

29. Many councils have also established other agencies to shore up

their race-relations committees. In 1982, for example, Camden set up five working parties on specific topics, each of which had to report to the Race Relations Committee. Two of these still survive. Again individual council departments – particularly housing and social services – are also usually awash with race-relations working parties and sub-groups. Race and housing forums bring together council officers, council members, housing department race-relations advisers, housing organizations and black groups. Equally, Hackney's social services department, for example, has set up a policy/advisory group, a Social Needs Steering Group, a Social Services Race Panel, a Welfare Needs Group, a Research Interest Group and a Social Services Black Caucus. All either deal ex- clusively with black issues or have a large input from the black community.

30. Editorial, *Race Today*, January 1986.

31. Letter from W. A. McKee, chief executive, London Borough of Merton, *Guardian*, 14 October 1986.

32. In Hackney, for example, a large number of black community groups have been rocked by corruption scandals. Of course, graft has always been vital to the race-relations industry, to the extent that it has often been encouraged by councils themselves. Today, however, Hackney is anxious to expose frauds and incompetence on the part of black community groups – so as to close these down. The council has openly admitted that it has failed to monitor community groups in a professional manner: it has thus established a new council audit section, called in the district auditor to investigate matters and invited the Fraud Squad to investigate the Hackney Asian Association.

The confidence with which Hackney has gone on the offensive against black groups shows its success in raising a layer of obsequiously loyal black activists. Indeed, Hackney uses black activists themselves to monitor their former colleagues. This must count as one of the race-relations industry's greatest successes.

33. *Daily Telegraph*, 9 December 1983.

34. *Guardian*, 22 February 1984.

35. *London Evening Standard*, 8 August 1985.

36. *Daily Telegraph*, 14 September 1985.

37. *Voice*, 4 February 1984.

38. *Daily Telegraph*, 11 October 1984.

39. *Sun*, 20 February 1986.

40. *Morning Star*, 18 September 1985.

41. *The Times*, 15 February 1988.

42. Anthony Rampton (chairman), *Report of the Committee of Inquiry into the Education of Children from Ethnic Minority Groups*, HMSO, 1981.

43. ILEA, *Race, Sex and Class*, No. 2: 'Multi Ethnic Education in Schools', 1983.

44. ILEA, *Anti-Racist Statement*, August 1983.

45. Camden Council for Community Relations, *ILEA's Anti-racist Policy: What it Is: What it Will Do, How it Should Work*, CCCR, 1984.

46. *The Scarman Report*.

47. GLC Ethnic Minorities Committee, *Proposals for Special Programme of Anti-racist Activities 1983–84*, Report EM 104, June 1982.

48. GLC Ethnic Minorities Committee, *Anti-racist Programme of Activities 1983–85: Objectives and Outline Working Arrangements*, Report EM 270, 10 May 1983.

49. ibid.

50. ibid.

51. ibid.

52. ibid.

53. Ousley, 'Local Authority Race Initiatives', p. 171.

54. ibid.

55. ILEA, *Race, Sex and Class*, No. 3, 1983.

56. In the mid 1960s the USA was rocked by growing black militancy. From the Harlem revolt of 1964 to the rioting that shook 125 cities after Martin Luther King was assassinated in 1968, black communities acted to protect themselves. The US establishment's response was to send in the troops – and to set up special inquiries into the causes of the riots.

The Kerner Commission in 1968 and the US Commission on

Civil Rights in 1970 both admitted that racism was a 'white problem'. According to Kerner, the riots were 'in large part the culmination of 300 years of prejudice'. 'What white Americans have never understood,' wrote Kerner, 'is that white society is deeply implicated in the ghetto.' Likewise the Civil Rights Commission defined racism as 'any attitude, action or institutional structure which subordinates a person or group because of his or their colour'.

Beneath the radical language lay a more sober message: the American state bore no responsibility for racial oppression. Racism as a 'white problem' was a phrase borrowed from the Black Power movement. For black radicals it meant that oppression was the product of (white-dominated) American capitalism; for Kerner and others it meant that racism was the work of the white individuals.

Indeed, racism was held to be contrary to the American way of life. Gunnar Myrdal, the liberal social scientist, had already drawn attention to the conflict between 'American ideals of equality, freedom, God-given dignity of the individual, inalienable rights' and 'the practices of discrimination, humiliation, insult, denial of opportunities to Negroes and others in a racist society'. The new breed of anti-racists tried to resolve this conflict by 'changing the behaviour of whites'. The Civil Rights Commission made a distinction between 'overt racism' and 'indirect subordination': the latter was regarded as central to the tackling of racism, since it resulted from prejudices 'deeply embedded in white people from a very early age', prejudices that were also maintained through a racist 'cultural and belief system'. As Kerner put it, 'Whites need to understand the ghetto.'

Judy Katz, a prominent American educationalist, identified the logic that underlay this concept of racism. For Katz racism was a psychological problem – indeed, it was the 'number one mental health problem in the United States'. 'The disease of racism runs deeply through every white citizen,' she wrote. 'Because reality is distorted when one is mentally ill, there is difficulty in coping with reality.'

With racism conceived as a branch of insanity, anti-racism meant therapy and education. Therapy came in the form of 'racism-awareness training', which confronted individuals with their own prejudices. At the same time campaigns were launched to teach whites about black culture and to root racism out of American culture. The Chicago Campaign for One Society produced an 'Inventory of

Racism', which taught people how to look for the institutional sort. Educationalists, in particular, set up initiatives to improve both the image of blacks and the behaviour of whites. Patricia Bidol, Michigan's school superintendent, produced a very influential 'multimedia social studies curriculum' for the teaching of race relations at secondary level. The GLC went so far as to send members of its Ethnic Minority Unit to the USA to bring back US experiences such as these.

The GLC echoed, a decade after she first wrote it, Bidol's definition of racism – 'prejudice plus institutional power'. As for Katz, her 'Systematic Handbook of Exercises for the Re-education of White People with Respect to Attitudes and Behaviourism' is today the Bible of race-relations training in Britain.

57. As with racism-awareness training, the municipal anti-racists took the notion of multi-cultural education from the liberal integrationist movement in the USA.

58. Quoted in A. Sivanandan, 'RAT and the Degradation of the Black Struggle', *Race and Class*, vol. 26, no. 4, 1985.

59. For a full discussion on Dewsbury and its implications see Kennan Malik, 'The British School of Racism,' *The Next Step*, 18 September 1987.

60. Hackney Council, *Headcount*, 1985.

61. *Labour Research*, May 1986.

62. Spitalfields Housing and Planning Rights Service, *Bengalis and GLC Housing Allocation in E1*, 1982.

63. ibid.

64. Spitalfields Housing and Planning Rights Service, *Bengalis and GLC Housing Allocation in E1: An Update Report*, 1984.

65. ibid.

66. Figures from an internal Housing Department paper, quoted in *The Next Step*, 22 August 1986.

67. ibid.

68. ibid.

69. Because of Newham's multiplying homeless, the council has given priority to housing them: homeless people, predominantly white, now receive ninety of the 100 lets that are on average made

available each month. As a result, sixty black families in Canning Town alone just have to sit tight, wondering how many more attacks on their homes will be perpetrated before they finally move.

70. ibid.

71. Commission for Racial Equality, *Living in Terror*, London, 1987, p. 14.

72. *West Indian World*, 10 October 1984.

73. Hackney Council internal memorandum, 1986.

74. Islington Council, Housing Committee Minutes, September 1986.

75. For more information see *The Next Step*, 9 October 1987, p. 4.

76. At the start of the autumn term in 1985, during the final year of Conservative rule, there were eighty-nine vacant posts in Brent schools. By the spring of 1986, 1,500 children in Brent received only part-time education. Labour came to power in May, promising to reverse any school cuts imposed by the previous administration. Three months later, however, matters were even worse than under the Conservatives. There were now 172 vacancies – almost double the number of the year before. Twelve schools were without heads, and the average time for posts to be filled had risen to more than four months. (Figures taken from Brent Council Education Committee Minutes.)

5   A new anti-racist movement

1. *The Next Step*, 20 September 1985, p. 2.

2. *Guardian*, 30 October 1987.

3. David Cook *et al.* in *Marxism Today*, January 1988.

4. In its nine years of existence WAR has had considerable experience of fighting to win support for the defence of the victims of racial violence. Nasreen Saddique and her family are just one of many cases. For our efforts we have often been described as 'vigilantes' and have been criticized for being outsiders resorting to the same methods as the racists. Those employed in the race-relations industry seem to take particular exception to our work.

WAR has never been a vigilante movement of 'outsiders'. However, we do not believe that it is fruitful to expect the police to deal with racial violence. We believe that only locally based anti-racists can be relied upon to defend those under attack. Our strategy is based on a simple truth: that those responsible for racial violence are always a small minority and that, as such, they can be isolated if the majority of the community is mobilized behind those under attack.

Our aims in every situation are, first, to alert those who are appalled by racial violence to what is happening and to organize them to take a stand; and second, to explain to those who don't care why they should and why they too should take a stand. How we fulfil these aims depends on the situation. Sometimes we fix fire-proof letterboxes to the insides of doors, thereby saving lives. Sometimes we sit in the homes of those consistently subject to attack in order to give them confidence and to prove that they are not alone. Sometimes we confront the perpetrators of an attack with force. There can be no blueprint for dealing with racial violence, for every situation is specific. However, there is one over-riding principle – that the victim's safety must be the most important factor in determining our response.

In all cases we begin by ensuring that we know who the attackers are. Then it is often enough merely to be on hand when an attack is about to be carried out for the attackers to desist. The possibility of opposition is a constant factor that makes racists think twice about proceeding. More frequently than not, they are cowards – people who will attack only an unprotected and weak opponent. Here W A R's mere presence solves the problem.

W A R cannot always nip an attack in the bud. That is why it is crucial to involve the local community in protecting black people. To be sure that neighbours and local residents are aware of what is happening, we canvas door to door, asking people about their views on immigration and racism. When we identify anti-racists we discuss what is happening with them and, before long, get to know those people who are prepared to do something about it. In this way we begin the process of successfully isolating the attackers.

5. George Roucou, speaking in Manchester Town Hall, 26 November 1986.

6. Interview with W A R, 3 April 1987.

7. Letter to W A R from David Graham, chair of the George Roucou Defence Campaign, 4 April 1987.

8. Letter from the Home Office to Metso Moncrieffe, 21 August 1984.

9. Interview with WAR, 11 September 1987.

Further reading

There is a wealth of written material on racism. Here is some of the most useful reading for those interested in doing something about the issue.

Regular publications

The *Caribbean Times* and the *Asian Times* are news weeklies covering developments in the West Indian and Asian communities.

Race Today, published by the Race Today Collective, and *Race and Class*, published by the Institute of Race Relations, are radical journals carrying discussion of current developments in racism and the response to it.

The Next Step, weekly newspaper of the Revolutionary Communist Party, includes all Workers Against Racism theoretical and agitational material.

The *Runnymede Trust Bulletin* is published monthly and includes coverage of all important developments in the race field.

The *Department of Employment Gazette* often covers discrimination in the job market.

The Office of Population and Census Surveys' *Monitor* carries information regarding the state of the black community in terms of housing, education, etc.

Books

Muhammad Anwar, *Race and Politics*, Tavistock, London, 1986.
Peter Fryer, *Staying Power*, Pluto Press, reprinted 1988.
Zig Layton Henry, *The Politics of Race in Britain*, Allen and Unwin, London, 1984.
A. Phizacklea and R. Miles, *Labour and Racism*, Routledge and Kegan Paul, London, 1980.
The Roots of Racism, Junius Publications, London, 1985.

Reports and surveys

Report of the Findings of the Independent Inquiry, Roach Family Support Campaign, 1988.
Racial Attacks: Report of a Home Office Study, HMSO, 1981.
Policing Against Black People, Institute of Race Relations, 1987.
Living in Terror, Commission for Racial Equality, 1987.
Lord Gifford, QC, *et al.*, *Report of the Independent Inquiry into the Broadwater Farm*, Broadwater Farm Youth Association, 1986.

Index

activists
  councils and, 111
  under GLC anti-racism, 100–102, 104
  as 'representatives', 105, 106, 107
Acts of Parliament
  Commonwealth Immigrants (1962), 66–7, 68, 161
  Housing (Homeless Persons) (1977), 82
  Immigration (1971, 1987), 60–61, 69, 163
  Nationality (1948, 1981, 1983), 75–7, 164
  Police and Criminal Evidence, 134
  Public Order, 134
  Race Relations (1965, 1975), 93
Advisory Committee for Multicultural Education, 46
Africa, immigration from, 158, 161
Afro-Caribbeans see West Indians
Alfred Herbert factory, 72
Ali, Altab, xix, 107
Ali, Ishaque, xix
Ali, Mr, xiii, 139–41
Allen, P C, 36
Amnesty International, report on Broadwater Farm, 35
Amory, Merle, 110
Anklesaria, Kayimarz, xix
anti-immigrant bipartisanship, 69–71
anti-nationalism, 137–9
Anti-Nazi League, 3

anti-racism
  municipal, 99, 112–28; and cuts, 128–31; foundation and dynamics, 97–112; in London, 102–9
  new movement of, 134–53; manifesto for, 154–7
'anti-racist adviser', child, 113
Anti-racist Committee of Asians in East London, 107
anti-racist groups, 108
Anti-racist Strategies Team, 116
Arts and Recreation Committee, 103
Asians
  attacks on, xix, 79
  harassment of, 10–11, 17; police recruits, 34
  housing discrimination against, 86
  illegal immigrants, 80
  Immigration Bill and, ix
  immigration statistics, 161–2, 164–5
  Kenyan/Ugandan emigration, 68–9, 69–70
  percentage born in UK, 166
  refusal of benefits to, 81–2
  unemployment among, 85
  union discrimination against, 73
  virginity testing of brides, 70
  visitor visas for, 78–9
  workers' strike, 73
attacks
  police, 21–2; in Broadwater Farm affair, 43–5
  by racists: British response to, 139; Conservative policy on, 109; municipal failures over,

FOR THE BEST IN PAPERBACKS, LOOK FOR THE

In every corner of the world, on every subject under the sun, Penguin represents quality and variety – the very best in publishing today.

For complete information about books available from Penguin – including Pelicans, Puffins, Peregrines and Penguin Classics – and how to order them, write to us at the appropriate address below. Please note that for copyright reasons the selection of books varies from country to country.

In the United Kingdom: For a complete list of books available from Penguin in the U.K., please write to *Dept E.P., Penguin Books Ltd, Harmondsworth, Middlesex, UB7 0DA*

In the United States: For a complete list of books available from Penguin in the U.S., please write to *Dept BA, Penguin, 299 Murray Hill Parkway, East Rutherford, New Jersey 07073*

In Canada: For a complete list of books available from Penguin in Canada, please write to *Penguin Books Canada Ltd, 2801 John Street, Markham, Ontario L3R 1B4*

In Australia: For a complete list of books available from Penguin in Australia, please write to the *Marketing Department, Penguin Books Australia Ltd, P.O. Box 257, Ringwood, Victoria 3134*

In New Zealand: For a complete list of books available from Penguin in New Zealand, please write to the *Marketing Department, Penguin Books (NZ) Ltd, Private Bag, Takapuna, Auckland 9*

In India: For a complete list of books available from Penguin, please write to *Penguin Overseas Ltd, 706 Eros Apartments, 56 Nehru Place, New Delhi, 110019*

In Holland: For a complete list of books available from Penguin in Holland, please write to *Penguin Books Nederland B.V., Postbus 195, NL–1380AD Weesp, Netherlands*

In Germany: For a complete list of books available from Penguin, please write to *Penguin Books Ltd, Friedrichstrasse 10 – 12, D–6000 Frankfurt Main 1, Federal Republic of Germany*

In Spain: For a complete list of books available from Penguin in Spain, please write to *Longman Penguin España, Calle San Nicolas 15, E–28013 Madrid, Spain*

A CHOICE OF PENGUINS AND PELICANS

The Second World War (6 volumes)   Winston S. Churchill

The definitive history of the cataclysm which swept the world for the second time in thirty years.

1917: The Russian Revolutions and the Origins of Present-Day Communism
Leonard Schapiro

A superb narrative history of one of the greatest episodes in modern history by one of our greatest historians.

Imperial Spain 1496–1716   J. H. Elliot

A brilliant modern study of the sudden rise of a barren and isolated country to be the greatest power on earth, and of its equally sudden decline. 'Outstandingly good' – *Daily Telegraph*

Joan of Arc: The Image of Female Heroism   Marina Warner

'A profound book, about human history in general and the place of women in it' – Christopher Hill

Man and the Natural World: Changing Attitudes in England 1500–1800
Keith Thomas

'A delight to read and a pleasure to own' – Auberon Waugh in the *Sunday Telegraph*

The Making of the English Working Class   E. P. Thompson

Probably the most imaginative – and the most famous – post-war work of English social history.

FOR THE BEST IN PAPERBACKS, LOOK FOR THE 🐧

A CHOICE OF PENGUINS AND PELICANS

The French Revolution Christopher Hibbert

'One of the best accounts of the Revolution that I know . . . Mr Hibbert is outstanding' – J. H. Plumb in the *Sunday Telegraph*

The Germans Gordon A. Craig

An intimate study of a complex and fascinating nation by 'one of the ablest and most distinguished American historians of modern Germany' – Hugh Trevor-Roper

Ireland: A Positive Proposal Kevin Boyle and Tom Hadden

A timely and realistic book on Northern Ireland which explains the historical context – and offers a practical and coherent set of proposals which could actually work.

A History of Venice John Julius Norwich

'Lord Norwich has loved and understood Venice as well as any other Englishman has ever done' – Peter Levi in the *Sunday Times*

Montaillou: Cathars and Catholics in a French Village 1294–1324
Emmanuel Le Roy Ladurie

'A classic adventure in eavesdropping across time' – Michael Ratcliffe in *The Times*

Star Wars E. P. Thompson and others

Is Star Wars a serious defence strategy or just a science fiction fantasy? This major book sets out all the arguments and makes an unanswerable case *against* Star Wars.

FOR THE BEST IN PAPERBACKS, LOOK FOR THE 🐧

A CHOICE OF PENGUINS AND PELICANS

Lateral Thinking for Management   Edward de Bono

Creativity and lateral thinking can work together for managers in developing new products or ideas; Edward de Bono shows how.

Understanding Organizations   Charles B. Handy

Of practical as well as theoretical interest, this book shows how general concepts can help solve specific organizational problems.

The Art of Japanese Management   Richard Tanner Pascale and Anthony G. Athos   With an Introduction by Sir Peter Parker

Japanese industrial success owes much to Japanese management techniques, which we in the West neglect at our peril. The lessons are set out in this important book.

My Years with General Motors   Alfred P. Sloan   With an Introduction by John Egan

A business classic by the man who took General Motors to the top – and kept them there for decades.

Introducing Management   Ken Elliott and Peter Lawrence (eds.)

An important and comprehensive collection of texts on modern management which draw some provocative conclusions.

English Culture and the Decline of the Industrial Spirit   Martin J. Wiener

A major analysis of why the 'world's first industrial nation has never been comfortable with industrialism'. 'Very persuasive' – Anthony Sampson in the *Observer*

A CHOICE OF PENGUINS AND PELICANS

Dinosaur and Co   Tom Lloyd

A lively and optimistic survey of a new breed of businessmen who are breaking away from huge companies to form dynamic enterprises in microelectronics, biotechnology and other developing areas.

The Money Machine: How the City Works   Philip Coggan

How are the big deals made? Which are the institutions that *really* matter? What causes the pound to rise or interest rates to fall? This book provides clear and concise answers to these and many other money-related questions.

Parkinson's Law   C. Northcote Parkinson

'Work expands so as to fill the time available for its completion': that law underlies this 'extraordinarily funny and witty book' (Stephen Potter in the *Sunday Times*) which also makes some painfully serious points for those in business or the Civil Service.

Debt and Danger   Harold Lever and Christopher Huhne

The international debt crisis was brought about by Western bankers in search of quick profit and is now one of our most pressing problems. This book looks at the background and shows what we must do to avoid disaster.

Lloyd's Bank Tax Guide 1987/8

Cut through the complexities! Work the system in *your* favour! Don't pay a penny more than you have to! Written for anyone who has to deal with personal tax, this up-to-date and concise new handbook includes all the important changes in this year's budget.

The Spirit of Enterprise   George Gilder

A lucidly written and excitingly argued defence of capitalism and the role of the entrepreneur within it.